FOREWORD

One of the unsolved problems of Curriculum Development is how to bring about the dissemination of new ideas, especially new ideas from expensive and elaborate curriculum projects. David Whitehead, who is best known as an expert on the teaching of Economics in schools, looks at the general question of dissemination, and in greater detail at the attempt to spread the good news about one particular project – the *Schools Council History, Geography and Social Science 8-13 Project.*

Various models of diffusion and dissemination are examined and many found wanting both at the theoretical and practical levels. A number of projects are referred to, but probably the most interesting aspect of this research is a detailed case study of HGSS. David Whitehead looks at this project from the point of view of a sympathetic economist; he examines the project philosophy, the kinds of publications produced for teachers, and, finally, investigates how the materials are actually being used in schools. The results are extremely disturbing, perhaps even startling. What went wrong? What lessons can be learned? Mr Whitehead concludes by attempting to answer these questions as well.

All this adds up to a very interesting and penetrating analysis of curriculum development. It was written before the Schools Council's own analysis was produced (the Impact and Take-up project) but the interim report on that project is summarised in chapter IX.

Mr Whitehead's book is a very important addition to the *Curriculum Research Papers* both from a theoretical and a practical point of view.

Denis Lawton

CONTENTS

The Dissemination of Educational Innovations in Britain

David J Whitehead

HODDER AND STOUGHTON
LONDON SYDNEY AUCKLAND TORONTO

ACKNOWLEDGMENTS

I would like to express my warm
appreciation of the encouragement I have
received from Professor Denis Lawton.
Other colleagues who have given me
invaluable advice include Linda Thomas,
Richard Pring, Peter Gordon and Helen
Simons.
Hazel Sumner initially stimulated my
interest in this field of curriculum studies.
Sarah Whitehead's scrupulous reading of
the manuscript helped to eliminate
unnecessary jargon and stylistic infelicities.
All remaining faults must as usual be
attributed to the author.

Whitehead, David, *b. 1943*

The dissemination of educational innovations in
Britain.
1. Schools Council Project History, Geography
and Social Science 8–13
2. Curriculum planning – Great Britain
3. Educational innovations – Great Britain
I. Title.
375'.001   LB1564.G7

ISBN 0 340 24444 5

Printed in Great Britain for Hodder and Stoughton Educational,
a division of Hodder and Stoughton Ltd,
Mill Road, Dunton Green, Sevenoaks, Kent,
by J.W. Arrowsmith Ltd, Bristol.

INTRODUCTION

Most teachers trained since the Second World War have been exposed to courses expounding the 'educational disciplines' — philosophy, psychology and sociology of education plus the historical and comparative dimensions. By the end of the 1960s, increasing numbers of teachers in training were questioning whether their initiation into these fields of knowledge was sufficiently worthwhile. Meanwhile, rumblings of discontent with the school curriculum had manifested themselves in the appearance of projects, often sponsored by charitable foundations, which could not easily be examined within the academic boxes created by education departments. As curriculum development progressed during the 1960s, the official stamp of approval on such activity was given by the creation of the Schools Council in 1964. Henceforth most innovation would be channelled through, and financed by, an 'accrediting' institution.

By the late 1960s, some student teachers were given a little information about the Schools Council and its functions, but even by 1978, students at the end of their professional training could be found who had not been told about important curriculum development projects in their own subject fields. Little wonder that the 1978 Schools Council Report: 'Impact and Take-up Project' showed that ignorance of the Schools Council and of projects under its aegis was widespread (see chapter IX).

Some progress has been made with the setting up of curriculum studies departments, providing a forum for the critical examination of the large variety of new materials and methods offered on the educational market. But by the middle-1970s, it had come to be realised that it was insufficient just to scrutinize Schools Council Projects and their materials and new methods, fresh from Great Portland Street. A medicine can be tested in the laboratory, and found very effective. But what if the patient won't take it, or doesn't know it exists? So the focus of attention began to shift to whether the projects were being implemented in the schools, and if so, how. Such research resulted in findings which dismayed curriculum developers.

Kerr notes that, in the early '60s, it was maintained that 'at the practical and organisational levels, the new curricula promise to revolutionise English education'.[1] In those heady days, it was widely assumed that curriculum innovations would succeed on their self-evident or evaluated merits, and would be gratefully accepted by the schools.[2] But such predictions soon came to be seen as unrealistic. After-sales service, or treatment for post-operative shock, was seen to be essential for long-term survival. Hence interest began to centre on what could be done to ensure that teachers would hear about Projects, and what diffusion methods might be effective.

Initially, critics of the Schools Council had viewed it as a machine whose products would infiltrate the curriculum and reduce local (that is teachers') control of it. A decade later, radicals complained of its ineffectual marketing techniques (and philosophy); conservatives were pleased that it had had practically no influence on the curriculum at all. Where the 'products' *had* been bought, investigations in the schools showed that either teachers were not properly reading the instructions in the packages, or that they were using the materials as they saw fit, regardless of the intentions of the developers.

This conclusion is neatly summarised by Herron: 'For nearly two decades now, we have seen large amounts of capital invested in the production of a wide variety of new curricula. Unfortunately, evidence is beginning to accumulate that indicates that much of this effort has had relatively little impact on the daily routine of the average classroom teacher. A grant expires and an outside consultant or team leaves the scene. The common occurrence is of the new program or project being introduced into a school system and then disappearing without trace.'[3] Kelly makes a similar point: 'Because curriculum projects are invariably limited in time by funds and resources, the subsequent implementation of their work other than in trial schools has tended to be uncontrolled, variable and inevitably less than was hoped.'[4]

Project teams unquestionably learned how to manage the development of new materials and methods. Unfortunately, neither they nor the Schools Council realised how great would be the difficulties of effecting even a minimal change in the school curriculum. Gradually, as information began to filter back via publishers and others to developers, it became apparent that a large number of projects had only been taken up on a very small scale. Consequently, project teams began to devote more thought (and more time and money, if they had them) to problems of dissemination, and their concern was reflected in a Schools Council report on dissemination published in 1973.[5]

Once a project team was appointed, it was normal practice for it to decide its own strategy, and this would usually include some provision for dissemination towards the end of the project's life. Each project chose its own approach, and the diversity of methods used meant that it was difficult to assess which were the more effective, and where the Schools Council might give more systematic assistance.[6]

What usually happened, up to the early 1970s, was for a project to realise, as it approached the end of its life, that it had not devoted enough time, thought and resources to the dissemination phase, and it would consequently ask for and obtain in some form an extension of its life. Often only some of the project team would stay for this additional period, the resources devoted to it would be too limited and the time available would be too short. For example, the Science 5-13 Project was permitted a two-year period of dissemination and 'after-care' from 1973-5 but, according to the Schools Council, further work still needed to be done. Such extensions to project lives proved expensive but not particularly successful, so elements within the Schools Council began to press for a more effective policy on dissemination. Their comments were reinforced by feedback from Teachers' Centres wardens, who were often very unhappy about many aspects of project dissemination. One possible solution lay in project dissemination via in-service training, an idea which was consonant with the proposals of the James Report on Teacher Education and Training, and the White Paper *Education: A Framework for Expansion.*

This analysis of the diffusion of innovations begins with an examination of some leading exponents' views on the dissemination process. These models are then used to highlight the salient features of the History, Geography and Social Science (HGSS) 8-13 Project. Next, an assortment of possible dissemination strategies are suggested, and the crucial role of the teacher discussed. Models derived from curriculum evaluators are proposed for assessing the effectiveness of particular dissemination techniques.

The next chapter investigates the dissemination strategy of the HGSS 8-13 Project Team, and is followed by a more general discussion of the use of packaged kits in curriculum development. Results of a survey on the take-up of the HGSS 8-13 Project generate some hypotheses about how methods of diffusion might be improved. Finally, other evidence is drawn together concerning the dissemination of educational innovations, and some personal reflections put forward for future curriculum developers to consider.

References

1 Kerr, J.F. (ed.), *Changing the Curriculum* (University of London Press Ltd, 1968), p.15.
2 MacDonald, B. and Walker, R., *Changing the Curriculum* (Open Books, 1976), see Chapter 2 *passim.*
3 *Schools Council Working Paper 56:* 'Dissemination of Innovation: The Humanities Curriculum Project' (Evans/Methuen Educational, 1976), p.13.
4 Kelly, P.J., 'The Process of Curriculum Innovation', pp.84-106 in *Paedagogica Europaea,* vol. VI, 1970/71.
5 *Schools Council Pamphlet 14:* 'Dissemination and In-service Training': Report of the Working Party on Dissemination 1972/3, pp.2-3.
6 ibid., p.3.

CHAPTER I

THREE VIEWS ON THE DISSEMINATION OF INNOVATIONS

Rudduck and Kelly

These writers isolate four main components in the dissemination process.[1] They call the first *Translocation,* and define it as the movements of people and materials necessary to implement new aspects of the curriculum. The kind of problems covered by this element include whether inspectors or members of project teams should visit teachers in schools, whether teachers should be encouraged to attend induction courses, whether people in different posts should be exchanged, and how packages of materials should be disseminated.

The second component, *Communication,* describes how information about an innovation is transmitted from one person to another. Central problems include the form which written communications should take, whether information might be broadcast through other channels, and to what extent personal interaction might be important in encouraging diffusion. Communication was a key element in the strategy of the Humanities Curriculum Project.[2] This Project considered it essential to build a communication and support system, in order to maintain its dynamism. Otherwise it might atrophy, as teachers changed their jobs, or no longer allocated resources to it, or began to use it wrongly, in ways not in line with the project's philosophy.

Rudduck and Kelly's third component, *Animation,* describes the need to arouse teachers' interest in the project, and to provide some motivation for them to involve themselves in it. It may be appropriate to provide some form of incentives. Certainly attitudes will need to be changed.

Their last component, *Re-education,* 'implies that considerable understanding and commitment are required in the effective implementation of an innovation'.[3] The implications are that regular training programmes will be essential, teachers will need to experiment with new projects in co-operation with one another, and good relations should be established between project teams and innovating teachers.

Rudduck and Kelly survey the strategies and experience of curriculum disseminators, and they reach the conclusion that Re-education has seldom been achieved, and that only recently has the importance of motivating teachers been appreciated. They consider that past neglect might be accounted for by concentration on changing the *content* of the curriculum. Emphasis now centred on the need for changing the way in which the teacher performed his role, since most new projects involved him in many unorthodox teaching techniques and other classroom activities.

Apart from these four major components of the dissemination process, these writers also suggest that it may be divided into three time phases. The first is *Receptivity,* which implies that organisations and teachers must be prepared (softened up?) for change. Sometimes this results from the same social changes which have stimulated the innovations, but it is often absent from project teams' strategies. The next phase is *Adoption,* during which the team aim to get the project taken up, or its new ideas received. Finally comes the *Implementation* phase, which is concerned with how the project is used in practice and how the innovative process is maintained. Not all projects display every phase; this depends on the nature of the project and its fundamental conceptual structure. Some projects, which were set up apart from, or just associated with, the mainstream of innovating educational agencies (such as the Business Studies Project), have until recently only tentatively ventured beyond the Receptivity phase, not wishing to be accused of trying to undermine teachers' or authorities' freedom of choice on the curriculum. Others, such as the Political Literacy Project, have displayed a sensitive awareness of the importance of the right sort of publicity.

Rudduck and Kelly conclude that 'the phases of dissemination are complementary to the components of dissemination. Each phase involves each of the components to some extent but not necessarily equally so. Thus, for example, Receptivity relies most on Communication and Animation. With Implementation, Re-education is of greatest significance.'[4]

The conceptual structure adopted by these writers is helpful in providing a framework within which particular curriculum development projects may be discussed. Their analysis of the components and phases of dissemination is however not prescriptive. It may be considered as a series of hypotheses, derived from their examination of success and failure in curriculum development, which have not yet been refuted. In contrast to the above model, which is not necessarily descriptive of actual processes, R. Havelock and D. Schon began by suggesting models which illuminated what they took to be the current theory of the dissemination of innovations. Subsequently they suggested other models which were less descriptive, but provided what they regarded as more helpful ways of considering how to disseminate.

Schon

This writer's views have received wide currency through his Reith Lectures. He distinguishes three models for the dissemination of innovations.[5]

(a) The Centre-Periphery Model
This model has three core elements: '1. The innovation to be diffused exists, fully realised in its essentials, prior to its diffusion. 2. Diffusion is the movement of an innovation from a centre out to its ultimate users. 3. Directed diffusion is a centrally managed process of dissemination, training and provision of resources and incentives.'[6]*

Admittedly Schon is more concerned with making general statements about the process of dissemination of *any* innovation, but the four factors which he isolates as critical to the effectiveness of a centre-periphery system can be applied to an *educational* dissemination of this kind. These are:

    (i)   the level of resources and energy at the centre,

---

* Apart from its use in this American quotation, the term 'dissemination' is taken to mean a planned phase of activity by the project team, while 'diffusion' refers to what happens after the life of a project.

(ii) the number of points at the periphery,

(iii) the length of the radii or spokes through which diffusion takes place, and

(iv) the energy required to gain a new adoption.

But in the United Kingdom none of these factors is particularly relevant, since the critical factor which has successfully prevented the effective application of the model is its inappropriateness. Although it may be possible to identify the typical curriculum development project as the 'centre' in this model, this is not justified, because in terms of power and permanence it is the schools and local education authorities which constitute the centre. The projects, and even the Schools Council, are 'marginal, precarious and temporary. The developers command no one and can afford to offend very few. They depend entirely upon the voluntary co-operation of system personnel, and have only a short time in which to ensure the survival of their work in schools and to secure their own personal futures.'[7] In other words, this model is not very helpful when applied to a system with dispersed decision-making about the curriculum.[8]

An amusing variant of this model is described by Schon. The 'centre' may be embodied in a kind of peripatetic bard (prophet or soothsayer?), roaming his territory to spread the good news. Some well-known leaders of curriculum development projects have cast themselves in this role. J. Bruner and L. Senesh are examples of prophets receiving at least as much honour in foreign parts. Miles points out that most innovative undertakings require considerable specialisation of role. 'Thus we have the agitator, the dreamer, the skillful *(sic)* navigator *vis-à-vis* the environment, and the internal administrator as recurring and presumably crucial roles. Another prominent role is that of the "committed nut" – the monomaniac, fanatic or "true believer".'[9]

(b) The Proliferation of Centres Model
Schon sees this as an elaboration of his first model, in which there are secondary as well as primary centres. 'Secondary centres engage in the diffusion of innovations; primary centres support and manage secondary centres ... the limits to the reach and effectiveness of the new system depend now on the primary centre's ability to generate support and manage the new centres.'[10]

A variant of this is the 'magnet model', where the main centre attracts disseminating agents, and attempts to manage the secondary centres' relations with their clients (the schools). 'The model ... makes of the primary centre a trainer of trainers. The central message includes not only the content of the innovation to be diffused, but a pre-established method for its diffusion. The primary centre now specialises in training, deployment, support, monitoring and management.'[11]

Schon suggests various reasons why this model may fail in application. First, he argues that 'when the network of communications of money, men, information and materials is inadequate to the demands imposed on it, the system must either retrench or fail ... the need for rapid central response, or for a more differentiated response to widely varying regional conditions, may overtax the available infrastructures.'[12]

Secondly, it may become evident that the main centre needs to develop its leadership and management role, but that it has insufficient resources to do so. Alternatively, the person acting as intermediary in the secondary centre may lack the incentive to

4

promote any particular project; his future is not brightened by the success of any one project.

It could be argued that this descriptive model is more relevant in the British context, since Teachers' Centres have been set up by local education authorities and encouraged by the Schools Council as local bases for dissemination of curriculum development projects. But Schon rightly cautions that the model's effectiveness is constrained by the power of the primary centres. In the United Kingdom the centres (the Project Teams) only stay together for four or five years at the most. Teachers' Centres, in contrast, are permanent, and are not beholden to the Project Teams, but to their employing authorities in each locality.

Another application of this model may be seen in the West German state of Bavaria.[13] Here the State Institute for School Education, set up in 1971, is the central innovating agency. This body revises curriculum guidelines, which largely prescribe the objectives and content of learning. It also gives educational support to and evaluates school trials, and plans an overall in-service training programme. The Institute sets up central working parties of teachers in charge of particular subjects, and co-ordinates their work. These groups prepare drafts for curriculum guidelines, as well as teacher guides and exemplar curriculum units. All plans and materials are tested in selected trial schools, and the process is monitored by an extension evaluation programme which is fed back into a revision of the drafts. If the Education Ministry agrees to the proposals, a separate programme is launched — the dissemination of the final products. The original working parties plus University staff then train so-called 'multiplicators', who are in turn responsible for inducting teachers into the new guidelines at the regional level.

(c) The Periphery-Centre Model[14]

As the title implies, the thrust is in the reverse direction to that in the first model. Problems are first encountered 'at the chalk face', and if it appears that innovation is needed, such information is disseminated to the central organisation which makes suggestions about how localised solutions may be reached. Sometimes this is described as a 'movement' model.

Rudduck and Kelly argue that Schon's first two models, which fairly accurately describe the models of dissemination followed in most countries, are essentially linear — ideas and resources are communicated from the development team to the teachers in the classroom. But the reason for including the third model is that project teams increasingly try to incorporate elements of it in their planning.

In particular, curriculum developers are realising that not only will more two-way communication be likely to result in improved ideas and materials, but it will also help to motivate the teacher. Thus the model is developing into one with cyclical elements, and the role of innovator is dispersed and shared. 'Wider understanding of the variety of agents and the complexity of their relationships in dissemination has also changed the model. It is now conceived much more as a web of relationships than a one-to-one relationship.'[15]

A complex example of how tangled such a web of relationships may become is demonstrated by the experience of the West German state of Hesse.[16] In establishing comprehensive schools, Hesse gave considerable freedom to the teachers involved to develop their own curricula (the 'movement' model). This grassroots approach was effective initially, when development was restricted to a few schools which had attracted able teachers who were keen to innovate. But as the number of schools involved increased, the problems of lack of communication between schools and the amount of work required became serious barriers. Various kinds of support groups were established, and, eventually a co-ordinating 'Curriculum Committee' was set up, and about 150 teachers from the innovating schools and Universities were asked to co-operate in developing new guidelines for comprehensive schools. Here we can see the periphery-centre model developing.

The main problem was how to reconcile the autonomy of the schools with the need for co-ordination. The Ministry of Education wanted faster and more effective changes, so it set up small working parties of teachers and subject specialists, who rapidly produced guidelines which were offered to the schools for a one-year experimental phase. Here perhaps the 'movement' approach was being discarded in favour of the more 'efficient' 'centre-periphery' approach. This soon developed into a variant of Schon's second model, as the Ministry set up six regional centres to provide support for teachers who were keen to co-operate with the experiment. The aim was now to initiate a continuous process of school-based curriculum development that would offer a worthwhile in-service education experience for larger numbers of teachers.

But Hesse was a 'progressive' education authority, so it had set up procedures by which teachers, students and parents could participate in educational decision-making. To the Minstry's chagrin, many teachers and parents did not want the curriculum experiment in their schools. Ironically, the innovators became victims of their own ideology.

Havelock

This writer groups models of dissemination under three heads: (a) Research, Development and Diffusion; (b) Social Interaction; (c) Problem Solving.

(a) The Research, Development and Diffusion (RDD) Model

This model, long established in agricultural research, was taken over in its entirety in the early stages of curriculum development, and is still often accepted as how dissemination does (or should) take place, where ideas and materials have to reach geographically dispersed users. Like Schon's earlier models, the RDD approach implies a straightforward linear progression from research to development to dissemination, final adoption being taken (too much) for granted. Lawrence Stenhouse describes how the first phase of curriculum innovation in the United Kingdom conformed to this model, and incorporated the Tyler/Bloom objectives approach. The output was obvious and clearcut: classroom materials and teacher handbooks.[17] However, Stenhouse proceeds to make the valid point that often projects depart from the RDD model on the assumption that it is products, rather than the hypotheses or ideas behind these products, which are being tested.

Another approach which has similarities to Havelock's is the Rostovian model developed by Shipman,[18] in which he suggests that planning curriculum changes is like giving aid to less developed countries. W.W. Rostow, the American economist, has shown how traditional societies may break into a stage of self-sustained economic growth by accumulating investment up to the point at which sufficient resources exist to generate further investment within the system. By analogy, it is hoped that the exogenous introduction of new ideas and materials to the schools will build up the momentum for them to take 'a great leap forward'.

However, perhaps schools, like under-developed countries (and Alice's Red Queen), have to run as fast as they can to stay in the same place. 'The breakthrough into self-sustained growth will depend on a combination of motivation to innovate by at least a minority and their ability to mobilise sufficient resources to introduce and sustain new methods, often in the face of opposition from groups supporting old procedures.'[19] But Shipman is pessimistic about the possibility of progress on these lines, since teaching, like work in under-developed countries, is so tiring that little energy remains for thought and action to change procedures. Teachers may be intent simply on survival, and they at least know that this is (just) possible if they continue working as they have always done. The frequent failure of investment programmes in less developed countries is paralleled by the failure of innovative programmes in the schools. Once the outside support and injection of ideas and resources are removed, the situation tends to revert to the *status quo ante*. This analysis does not however pertain to some centrally planned countries, where a greater degree of control is expected. If Shipman's analysis is right, then effective dissemination may imply the need for greater centralisation of decision-making over the curriculum to expedite change. However, it could be argued that his analogy is false since the assumption that schools *have* had considerable injections of investment in terms of new ideas and resources is invalid.

(b) The Social Interaction Model

In this composite model, Havelock stresses the communication of ideas rather than the distribution of materials. The approach has evolved from a reaction to the formalism of the RDD model, and the aim is to present a 'message' that will carry conviction, rather than evoke critical reaction and modification.

(c) The 'Problem-solving' Model

This approach starts from the needs of the school or teacher, and, as in Schon's 'movement' model, local needs are transmitted to curriculum developers, or they are diagnosed by local advisers or other 'change agents' and communicated back to the innovators. Feedback and co-operation are emphasized, with ideas flowing in both directions.

References

1   Rudduck, J. and Kelly, P., *The Dissemination of Curriculum Development* (NFER, 1976), p.98.

2   *Schools Council Working Paper 56:* 'Dissemination of Innovation: The Humanities Curriculum Project' (Evans/Methuen Educational, 1976), p.14.

3   Rudduck, J. and Kelly, P., ibid., p.99.

4   ibid., p.100.

5   Schon, D.A., *Beyond the Stable State* (Temple Smith, 1971).

6   ibid., p.81.

7   MacDonald, B. and Walker, R., *Changing the Curriculum* (Open Books, 1976), Chapter 3.

8   Munro, R.G., *Innovation: Success or Failure?* (Hodder and Stoughton Educational, 1977) p.44.

9   Miles, M.B., *Innovation in Education* (New York: Teachers' College, 1964), p.642.

10 Schon, D.A., ibid., p.85.

11 ibid., pp.85-6.

12 ibid., p.91.

13 Brugelmann, H., *Education for Teaching,* No. 98, Autumn 1975, 'Lost in the Desert of Innovation Theory — The Mirage of Dissemination and Implementation', pp.49-60.

14 Schon, D.A., ibid., p.110.

15 Rudduck, J. and Kelly, P., ibid., p.103.

16 See note 13 above, pp.51-2.

17 Stenhouse, L., *An Introduction to Curriculum Research and Development* (Heinemann Educational, 1975), p.219.

18 Shipman, M.D. with Bolam, D. and Jenkins, D., *Inside a Curriculum Project* (Methuen, 1974), p.122.

19 ibid., p.122.

CHAPTER II

CASE STUDY: DISSEMINATION MODELS
AND THE HISTORY, GEOGRAPHY
AND SOCIAL SCIENCE 8-13 PROJECT

It is evident from the publications of the History, Geography and Social Science (HGSS)* 8-13 Project that the project team did not espouse the classical models of curriculum dissemination expounded by Schon and Havelock and described in Chapter I. They placed much more emphasis on the 'movement' model, where the dissemination has no clearly established centre, but a variety of foci which expand and contract. Such a project also has no stable, centrally established 'message'. Rather, its doctrine is fluid and evolves.[1] The team held that curriculum development in its widest sense would be best served by such a process of dissemination. If all the dissemination points were linked by a communication network, then at least they all had the opportunity to learn from development elsewhere. Unfortunately, as will be seen later, the project team was never able to implement this philosophy, which could be characterised as 'teacher-centred dissemination'. They agreed that much of the literature on change in schools was pessimistic about the practical possibilities of teacher-centred dissemination. For example, Griffiths argues that the major impetus for change in organisations is from the outside and that when change in an organisation does occur, it will tend to be from the top down, not from the bottom

up.[2] Despite these caveats, the project team saw curriculum development as essentially about teacher education, and placed the major emphasis of the dissemination activity on teacher workshops rather than formal lectures.

In accordance with this model, the HGSS project team did hope to take a region of the United Kingdom, identify existing networks of teachers engaged with various parts of the project's curriculum area, and try to bring about some permanent linkage between them. Unfortunately the life of the project came to an end before this enterprise could be started.

One Teachers' Centre leader took the project's philosophy of diffusion to heart and developed the model of dissemination shown in Table I.[3] The crucial point is that schools (teachers) are central to this model, and the other agencies are focussed on the needs of the schools in developing their own curriculum. The movement in emphasis to the regional or local area means that the need for information and support for teachers developing project ideas becomes increasingly important. Martin argued that the network system set up by the Geography for the Young School Leaver (GYSL) Project, using regional and local co-ordinators and involving the LEAs, pointed the way to a method of closer local support for workshop groups of teachers

*At the time of going to press, a dissemination extension had just begun on this project.

and a means of exchanging information and ideas. His proposal for Regional Information Centres (RICs) and Regional Curriculum Development Centres (RCDCs) takes these ideas further. At the former, a teacher would be able to inspect the full range of materials and aids available, together with records of development work done locally or in other regions. The latter idea has already been implemented in Northumberland, where at Ponteland the Centre is stimulating development work by local groups in selected projects or area of the curriculum. (Three other centres have now been established.)

The RICs and RCDCs could co-operate in the area of resources, both facilitating distribution regionally and exchanging nationally. The Teachers' Centres would continue in this model and provide accessible bases for discussion and workshop groups. However, such a model has financial implications which make it impracticable in the present climate.

The team saw their role as essentially an amalgam of Havelock's 'social interaction' and 'problem solving' approaches. The HGSS 8-13 Project does put forward a Table of Objectives and Key Concepts (see page 41), but as the team's thinking progressed, members became increasingly aware of the significance of the *provisional* status of these suggestions. They came to see their role as 'initiating an on-going process of thinking. The Objectives and Key Concepts themselves, like the materials produced in the course of the Project's trials, acquire the role of exemplars, of what can constitute deep, reflective, systematic thought about the curriculum rather than the embodiment of what purports to be definitive wisdom.'[4] The project team's philosophy stressed particularly that no successful dissemination could take place without the teacher's role changing

considerably; in Rudduck and Kelly's terminology, Re-education was a vital ingredient. Blyth argued that the single aim was that teachers should think 'deeply, systematically and reflectively' about what they were doing and that this mental approach should become permanent. This was to have been the major goal of their dissemination programme, and the contribution that they were making to curriculum development in general.[5] Chapter VIII shows how far such goals were beginning to be achieved.

This team philosophy implied an ambivalent attitude towards the production of project materials. Certainly teachers might be given examples of what they might produce on applying their own objectives and concepts, but the team was suspicious of publishing voluminous and extremely good material which would tempt teachers to by-pass the analysis stage. As Blyth argues, 'it is not easy, when confronted with a dazzlingly complete set of materials and handbooks, to regard these as mere instances of what might be done. He would indeed be a bold and dedicated teacher who could realistically expect, in addition to his regular daily obligations, to rival in even a small measure the products of a project manned by an expert full-time team. With our emphasis on diffusion, we set out to avoid this outcome by institutionalising, from the outset, the context-specific nature of genuine curriculum process.'[6]

Although the project team appeared to reject the centre-periphery or proliferation of centre models, to an outside observer it seems that their actual dissemination strategy conformed quite closely to the latter model. This interpretation is reinforced by the description of the project's dissemination plans by Martin.[7]

The aim was to have five different levels of input from the Project Team, as follows:

(a) dissemination within existing trial schools;

(b) dissemination within trial areas to neighbouring schools using trial school teachers in the workshops;

(c) dissemination in a number of new areas where the project team organised workshops;

(d) dissemination in new areas where local co-ordinators after attending an induction course organised workshops supported by the Project Team;

(e) development of a system of contacts through which information on the Project could be broadcast so that groups and individuals are aware of others working locally on similar lines.

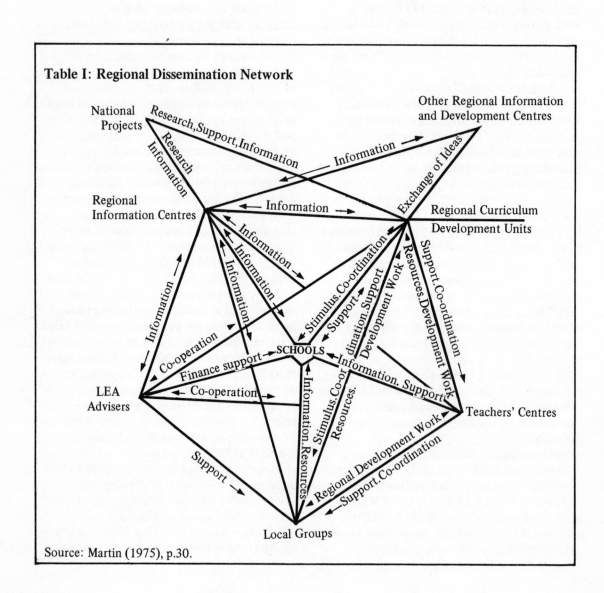

Table I: Regional Dissemination Network

Source: Martin (1975), p.30.

It may seem surprising that it was necessary to aim for dissemination within existing trial schools. This need was high-lighted at a conference where a number of geography teachers expressed interest in some games developed by the project. When they asked where they could see these operating, it was discovered that they were working at the same school in which the games had been in use for some time! Discussions were held with trial teachers about the possibility of spreading the project within the trial schools, but this was not in fact tried systematically in any of them.

Schon's analysis of the factors inhibiting a successful 'proliferation of centres' model may be applied here. His first factor is 'inadequate resources'. It may be supposed that the trial teachers were more enthusiastic in the trial phase than in the dissemination phase, since the former was accompanied by a substantial input of teaching materials and outside support. Another problem was that a number of teachers who had been involved in the trials were promoted at the end of the phase, or shortly afterwards. Also, particularly in primary schools, some teachers felt that they had concentrated too much on one aspect of their teaching, and that they now wanted to devote more time to other aspects. Finally, some of the trial teachers were devoting part of their spare time to helping dissemination in neighbouring schools — this might have been more exciting than the same activity pursued within their own schools.

The second level of dissemination was to be within the trial areas. However, only one such area had had any discussion about disseminating the project's ideas by the end of the trial phase.

The third type of dissemination was to be in new areas, with high project team involvement. Three areas were chosen, and the team concentrated especially on Wigan. The team spent much time explaining the project's ideas at teacher meetings. However, the commitment of the team, both in time and resources, could not last, and when the local advisers took over the momentum was lost. The impetus was also reduced by the problems caused by the re-organisation of local education authorities. In Cumberland, the schools involved remained essentially isolated, dependent on a direct link with the project team for ideas and support. No permanent structure for the project had been worked out by the time it came to an end, and it seemed probable that interest and involve-ment would fade away. The attempt to disseminate the project in a third area, Manchester, proved unsuccessful.

The next category was in new areas in which the project team would seek minimal involvement. Here success depended on the persistence of the local advisory team. whether there was much turnover of advisers, and the extent of disruption caused by re-organisation of local authorities.

Finally, it was intended to create a net-work in a large area (the West Midlands). However, in the end such a network was never seriously pursued by the project team. Instead, separate growth points within the area were encouraged. It was also hoped that dissemination would take place in areas which had displayed a spontaneous interest in the project. The way in which such dissemination took place is exemplified in the account of work in the Purbeck area referred to below.

The dissemination phase revealed two main constraints. First, there was the problem of allocating the senior research officers' time between dissemination work and preparation of materials for publication. Because the latter proved to be far more time-consuming than had been anticipated, it was not possible for the project team to devote as much time and energy to the dissemination work as had been hoped. Secondly, and related to the first problem, it was impossible to show materials at dissemination meetings, because of delays in publication. Although the team had an ambivalent attitude towards materials production, it was evident that many interested teachers were dissatisfied just to hear about project philosophy.

References

1 Schools Council History, Geography and Social Sciences 8-13 Project: *Project Conference Papers,* Homerton College, Cambridge, 4-6 April 1973, Part 4.
2 Miles, M.B., *Innovation in Education* (New York: Teachers' College, 1964), p.431, p.435.
3 Martin, K.A., 'Patterns of Dissemination. A Tale of Two Projects' (unpublished Mimeo, June 1975).
4 Schools Council, ibid., p.15.
5 Blyth, A., 'History, Geography and Social Science 8-13; a Second Generation Project', *The Curriculum: Research, Innovation and Change,* Taylor, P.H. and Walton, J. (eds.) (Ward Lock Educational, 1973), p.50.
6 ibid., p.48.
7 See note 3 above, p.16.

CHAPTER III

OTHER DISSEMINATION STRATEGIES

The most important statement on dissemination in recent years appears in a Schools Council Working Party Report; the main conclusions are summarised below.[1]

The Report argues that successful dissemination has taken place when teachers understand the project's ideas and materials sufficiently well to use them in school if they choose to do so. This implies that communications need to be improved to ensure that the information given by a project matches the requirements and increases the understanding of those receiving it. Teachers' choice should not be restricted by lack of organisational support. The Report maintains that although this definition of success is difficult to test, it is nevertheless a reasonable guide. It has to be accepted that very little can be measured in curriculum development. For example, sales figures of project materials give a very inadequate indication of how many are actually used (see Chapter VI). Even where teachers are using the materials, they may not be using them in the way in which the project intended. Moreover, sales figures do not give any indication of how many teachers are influenced by project philosophy even though they are not using its materials. Finally, some projects issue sample or inspection copy materials and, though not reflected in the sales figures, these may swell considerably the number of teachers coming into contact with a project.

In a section on criteria for dissemination strategy, the Report states quite blatantly that projects should follow a policy of positive promotion of their ideas and materials. This is in strong contrast to the rather discreet attitude which project directors have held in the past towards advertisement of their projects.

For example, the Humanities Curriculum Project (HCP) argued that a marketing approach which aimed to influence schools to purchase the 'package' should not be adopted. Rather, the dissemination programme should aim at providing information so that schools could make informed choices. However, the very existence of HCP packs of materials militated against the achievement of this aim, since it was commonly accepted that the materials *were* the project.[2] The language used by Tawney however implies a market relationship similar to that which the Schools Council Report had in mind '... ensure that the consumer is adequately and fairly informed ... providing information for the disseminator and for the adopter are two aspects of the same task, for in the long term it is likely that successful sales-manship depends on satisfied customers, who in turn depend on an accurate specification of the product and comprehensible directions for its use'.[3]

Success also depends on satisfied sellers. The speed with which an innovation is adopted is influenced by the speed or slow-ness with which publishers are able to produce and distribute relevant materials, and to continue to reap a regular profit from them. Publishers tend to over-emphasise novelty to try to increase sales. But they tend to *inhibit* later changes in the materials which would render obsolete or non-competitive materials that they have successfully launched and institutionalised.[4]

Another important role for the project team arises from the need to differentiate between the groups which it aims to influence, namely headteachers, teachers, teachers' centre wardens, education tutors and so on. It needs to predict how each group will respond to its work and establish and satisfy what each group requires in the way of information, participation and resources.

The team should consider the needs of potential adopters at each of the three broad stages of project development. The first stage is when teachers begin to become aware of the existence of the project and to show some interest in it. The project team could consider their efforts successful at this stage if teachers are aware of the project's aims and philosophy, its methods, its context (its place in the curriculum and for whom it is provided), its limitations and its proposed phasing. They should also know where further information may be obtained, where materials may be seen in use, and what implications the project has with regard to the amount of staff time, resources and accommodation that are required.

The Impact and Take-up Project throws some light on the important useful sources of information about projects for teachers. The eight most important sources were: teachers in the same school; teachers' centres and special resource centres; television for schools; short courses and conferences; the headteacher; teachers in other schools; book exhibitions; research journals and general books on education.

Perhaps the most surprising feature of this list is the relative importance of television as a source of information. On the other hand, specifically Schools Council sources hardly feature at all (though project information is probably seen at teachers' centres).

The main differences between teachers' rankings and those of headteachers is that the latter considered *Dialogue* (the now defunct Schools Council news bulletin) the second most important source of information. It may be that this publication did not feature in the teachers' list simply because it was not circulated and they did not see it.[5]

The main criteria for the second stage, that of trial and evaluation, are that trial schools should have all the draft materials, and should be familiar with project aims and philosophy, and that there should be a well-organised network of teacher groups' leaders to maintain teacher/project team two-way communication. It is sometimes suggested that the success of a project is correlated with the number of teachers from trial and associate schools who have been involved with it, and the Report suggests that in future it might be appropriate for projects to think in terms of accommodating all those schools which applied to participate, though such a policy would be very expensive.

The third stage is that of adoption or rejection, and it is here that, in the past, problems of dissemination have been most acute. Often the project team is dispersing by this time, and responsibility for carrying the 'good news' of the project is transferred to some other body. Success here depends very largely on the extent to which the project has organised, or encouraged the organisation of, a continuing training programme and local support systems which will outlive the project itself. Not only in-service training is needed, but also the inclusion of the project in the curriculum of some colleges and departments of education, and the opportunity (perhaps in teachers' centres) for teachers to discuss and adapt materials for local use.

The HCP team, for example, saw its dissemination in terms of providing opportunities for people to obtain adequate information about the project and what it entailed; of ensuring that there were enough well-run training courses; and of finding out what help teachers needed to continue the work set in motion by the project.[6] But the team also realized the necessity of weaning the schools from project support (given that its life was short). They had to get teachers, teachers' centre wardens, local authority advisers and college lecturers to take over responsibility for dissemination, and encourage them to develop relevant skills.

One conclusion which has emerged from all the evaluation studies of curriculum development projects is that the need for in-service education has always been underestimated.[7] This applies not only to the type of in-service course which is directly concerned with getting teachers to implement project strategies, but also to courses aimed at helping teachers to adapt innovations to their own needs.

Pre-service information is also important, as shown by the findings of the Impact and Take-up Project. Teachers were asked how they had found out about the project with which they were most familiar. Initial training was clearly the main first point of contact. 'Courses' (which included all kinds of in-service work) only figured to roughly the same extent as colleagues in the school in providing an introduction to the project.[8]

The flow of information about a project is often spasmodic, according to teachers' centre wardens, who say that once the honeymoon period of frequent contact with a project has elapsed, communication rapidly breaks down. For their part, the HCP team warned that the involvement of teachers' centre wardens in the dissemination of their project raised a number of issues that related to the status, competence and commitment of the centre leaders (the implication being that HCP was not totally satisfied with these intermediaries).[9]

The Report suggests as one remedy the appointment of liaison officers to act as points of contact in institutions in which they serve. Also, more information might be given through 'project profiles' and by the field officer team. As already stated, an experimental 'information centre' has been set up at Ponteland, to provide comprehensive and detailed information about curriculum development projects. The idea is that such a centre should be reasonably accessible to teachers, and in a setting associated with training and professional growth.

Another proposal put forward by the Report is that dissemination might be more successful if teachers were involved more intimately from the outset, particularly with regard to what projects should be run. This might increase the relevance of projects to classroom needs, hence reducing the problems of dissemination. It is difficult to see how more than a select number of teachers could be involved at the development stage, but the rest may during this phase be inducted by means of a HCP-type teacher training programme, or be given a set of training materials which would enable them to trace all the stages of the project's development, and undergo at one remove the modification of insights experienced by those actually involved. (See Watkins' ideas discussed in Chapter IV and the work of Wynne Harlen outlined in Chapter VII.)

The Report gives a great deal of practical

advice about what training materials should contain. First, general information should be provided about the project: its history, aims and objectives, philosophy and teaching strategy. Then there should be a sample kit, with introductory handbook, and tape recordings of interviews with the project director and of discussions with trial school teachers. Additional suggestions are a film, videotape or tape/slide sequence showing materials in use in the classroom, including discussion with pupils, and simulation exercises or problem-solving activities to involve a local teachers' group in the project's methods and approach. The training materials should deal with the implications of the project's adoption, in relation to other subjects, time-tabling, staffing and so on. They should contain units which lead teachers through the stages of development of the team's thinking, and other information of a supporting kind, such as the names of the project team, details of any after-care centres, any evaluation reports, and any contacts with other curriculum development projects.

Two other suggestions are made by the Report to enhance project dissemination. First, it seems that in the long run LEA support, and the extent to which the local education authorities are prepared to foster the development, will be crucial. Indeed, the HCP team asserted that their dissemination policy would only be effective if local authorities took responsibility for setting up some system for helping teachers interested in the project. They did not think it was possible to discern a uniform pattern of dissemination. In some areas, the project had disappeared for a time, but then re-emerged. Elsewhere, the local group of teachers involved with the project continued to provide active support, even when the composition of the group changed. In other places, the stimulus for setting up

in-service courses had come from individuals. In some instances, sporadic interest from dispersed schools had either persisted, or waned due to lack of organisational support.[10] Innovations certainly need local authority financial support. But an authority will often maintain that, because of lack of funds, it is unable to involve itself in curriculum dissemination.[11]

Secondly, with more advance planning project teams also might build contacts with radio, television and Open University programmes. This would meet the first criterion for a successful dissemination strategy mentioned above, which suggested that positive promotion of projects is needed.

The Impact and Take-up Project has shown how important the broadcasting media are as useful sources of information about projects. Television for schools was rated the second most *frequently* useful source, with BBC and ITV literature being placed fourth. The project concludes that 'either there is something in the nature of the provision or use of information from these media which prevents them serving to tell teachers about projects, or there is a potentially important channel available.'[12]

A paper produced by the Schools Council in March 1976 took up some of the ideas of the Working Party Report, which had been accepted by the Programme Committee.[13] A new point stressed by this paper is that there is a limit to the effectiveness of dissemination arrangements when a project's guides and other materials are not available at the start of the phase. In the past, the dissemination period has often been restricted to one year, and so for many projects the dissemination phase has ended well before the bulk of material has been published, and therefore well before the main build-up of requests from teachers for help, which tends to follow about a year after publication. Furthermore, if a project is one which provides suggestions for studies developing over a particular age range (for example, eight to thirteen years for the HGSS 8-13 Project), then in each successive year the teacher encounters a fresh set of new situations and unfamiliar problems, so support for teachers should be provided over these years. Hence dissemination and teacher support arrangements need to be maintained for a longer period if the project's intended outcomes are to be effectively achieved.[14]

Finally, the paper goes so far as to suggest that some past projects, which did not have a dissemination phase (amongst which it lists the HGSS 8-13 Project*), but which have been found to be of value and for which there is a demand for guidance, would still warrant a programme for dissemination and teacher support.

One project which benefited from the increased emphasis laid by the Schools Council on dissemination since 1972-3 was the Communication Skills in Early Childhood Project. While a grant was originally given for 1973-6, a sizeable sum was added so that a dissemination programme might be launched for 1976-8. Such an extension seemed desirable in view of the Impact and Take-up Project's finding that 49% of teachers of children aged 3-6 had not heard of the Early Childhood Project.[15]

The GYSL Project and the HGSS 8-13 Project — a comparison

Another way of considering project success is in terms of what conditions need to be met if a project is to be acceptable to the mass of teachers.[16] MacDonald and Walker

*This recommendation bore fruit in 1978. See page 38.

propose four desiderata: the project should be geared to the needs of the less able adolescent; it should take account of such pupils' limitations; it should allow teachers to decide how they are actually going to teach it; and its use should improve teachers' self-image and sense of professionalism. They proceed to argue that a project may only be successful (on a narrow definition of package sales) if it is able to conceal the considerable changes in classroom practice implied by its adoption.

The GYSL project has shown how effective dissemination strategy can be when implemented sensitively.[17] This project apparently succeeded where others, including the HGSS 8-13 Project, failed to be taken up. (GYSL achieved adoption in one-third of all secondary schools in fifteen months.) It is possible to distinguish between the characteristics of the two projects to try to highlight some of the reasons for the relative lack of success of the HGSS 8-13 Project.

A major difference between the two projects lies in the dissemination phase. Whilst the HGSS 8-13 Project could not achieve more than a truncated dissemination phase (see Chapter VI), the GYSL Project, initially financed for 1970-3, was extended for a further three years, one for materials editing and two for dissemination, with a full-time co-ordinator. In addition, whereas for HGSS 8-13 only a few local workshops were started, the GYSL Project created local curriculum groups in every LEA, with local and regional co-ordinators.

It is difficult to classify this distinction within the desiderata suggested by MacDonald and Walker for mass teacher acceptability. Yet it seems that the methodical and large-scale dissemination strategy pursued by the GYSL Project was a critical factor in its success. Certainly it offered a new insight into one part of the curriculum, suitable for average and less able 14-16 year olds. It thus satisfied a real need in secondary schools, compared with the HGSS Project, which was, especially with the Money Unit, trying to break into the market rather than just modernise an old product which exhibited substantial product loyalty. Connected with this was the attempt of the GYSL Project to establish close collaboration with external examination boards. The HGSS Project was not assessed externally, so any assessment of whether objectives had been achieved (if set) had to be generated by the teacher.

MacDonald and Walker next suggest that a project, if it is to be successful, should have a 'realistic' view of pupil's limitations. I am not competent to comment on the conceptual level of the GYSL Project, but from close scrutiny of the Money Unit of the HGSS 8-13 Project, it appears that this package was not too advanced for the pupils for which it was designed. However, whilst teachers of the former project presumably had had some training in Geography, very few teachers of the latter would have had any formal background in Economics. There is some evidence to suggest that teachers felt out of their depth (see Chapter VIII). In other words, take-up of some elements of the project may have been limited to some extent because of teachers' expectations that these elements might prove too difficult for them to handle.

The third criterion was that a project should respect teachers' autonomy concerning classroom practice. At dissemination conferences, the GYSL team stressed that adoption of the project did not necessitate revolution in classroom practices. Geography lessons and teachers already existed; it was just a change in emphasis and conceptual framework. But

for the HGSS 8-13 Project, social studies were certainly not time-tabled at all in many primary schools. Moreover, however much the project emphasised that units such as Money were to be conceived simply as exemplars, teachers without any academic background in Economics were unlikely to treat them as such. According to the Impact and Take-up Project, only 3% to 4% of primary school teachers had taken Social Science as a main subject during their college or university training. The philosophy of the project, entailing the introduction of key concepts and objectives, implied dissatisfaction with the existing rationale of classroom practice.

Lastly, MacDonald and Walker suggested that teachers were more likely to adopt a project if it reinforced their professional identity. Subject teachers in secondary schools have allegiance to their subject. If they are primarily sixth form teachers, this security is strong. Perhaps for subject teachers who teach mainly in the lower and middle school, this allegiance is more equivocal. A project such as GYSL strengthens their identification as geography teachers and enhances their status, being in the van of new curriculum developments in their subject. Primary and middle school teachers perhaps feel less subject allegiance, defining themselves simply as 'teachers' rather than as 'historians', 'geographers' and so on. Consequently a project such as HGSS 8-13 does not reinforce their professional identity. Any teacher perusing the materials would be made to feel guilty that he/she had not been adopting a conceptual approach, had not even been teaching some of these substantive concepts at all!

In conclusion, it appears that three of the four desiderata suggested by MacDonald and Walker are absent in the case of the HGSS 8-13 Project. It did not offer solutions tailored to the less able adolescent, it did not respect teachers' 'autonomy', and it did not reinforce teachers' professional identity. Above all, it lacked the rigorous and all-enveloping dissemination strategy of the GYSL Project.

References

1 *Schools Council Pamphlet 14:* 'Dissemination and In-service Training': Report of the Working Party on Dissemination 1972/3, *passim.*
2 *Schools Council Working Paper 56:* 'Dissemination of Innovation: The Humanities Curriculum Project' (Evans/Methuen Educational, 1976), p.14.
3 Tawney, D. (ed.), *Curriculum Evaluation Today: Trends and Implications,* Schools Council Research Studies (Macmillan, 1976), p.26.
4 Miles, M.B., *Innovation in Education* (New York: Teachers' College, 1964), p.641.
5 Steadman, S.D. *et al., Impact and Take-up Project:* Interim Report (Schools Council Mimeo, 1978), pp.76-9.
6 See note 2 above, p.19.
7 Eraut, M., 'Some recent evaluation studies of curriculum projects − a review', ibid., Tawney, D. (ed.), p.123.
8 Steadman, S.D. *et al.,* ibid., p.79.
9 See note 2 above, p.101.
10 ibid., p.37.
11 ibid., p.71.
12 Steadman, S.D. *et al.,* ibid., p.79 and p.84.
13 Schools Council, *Achieving Implementation of Projects:* Some conclusions from growing experience of dissemination and teacher support programmes, and some implications. Unpublished paper.
14 ibid., p.2.
15 Steadman, S.D. *et al.,* ibid., pp.36-7.
16 MacDonald, B. and Walker, R., *Changing the Curriculum* (Open Books, 1976), Chapter 3.
17 ibid., p.71.
18 Steadman, S.D. *et al.,* ibid., Appendix D, p.2.

CHAPTER IV

THE ROLE OF THE TEACHER IN THE
DISSEMINATION OF INNOVATION

It is evident that many of the recommenda-
tions of the Schools Council Working Party
Report on Dissemination are yet to be
implemented. What emerges from that
report are the enormous problems involved
in disseminating any innovation.[1] In
particular, what incentives are teachers to
be given to continue with their own
professional development, and how should
they be supported while doing so? To some
extent this problem will be alleviated by
teacher participation in national projects,
and with more appropriate provision of
initial and in-service training. Also, the
current aim of the Schools Council to
stimulate and support local, school-based
curriculum development should emphasise
the importance of the resourcefulness and
professionalism of the teacher. The
curriculum developer places an increased
workload on the innovating teacher, who
nevertheless often finds the participation
stimulating, especially when he is able to
improve the quality of any draft materials.
But this group of teachers, the 'high
innovators', is almost always small.[2]
'Converting the masses, euphemistically
referred to in the literature as dissemination,
requires more than the sowing of seed.'[3]

Often teachers buying project materials
have little or no experience of how they
have been developed, and so do not 'buy'
project philosophy. As stated above, stress
is now increasingly being laid on the teacher
as innovator, either in the narrow definition
as adaptor of innovations to local needs, or
as the originator in school-based curriculum
development.[4] This trend shows that
curriculum developers now realise the
crucial role that teachers play in the process
of innovation. They are no longer to be
considered just the passive recipients of
curriculum packages, but rather the focus
of curriculum development work,
contributing to dissemination as much as
receiving help because of it.

Many projects have required some change
in the way the teacher behaves in the classroom. It is unlikely that the teacher will
accept this unless he feels that he has
decided to effect such a change. Any implied
coercion to change his behaviour is very
likely to be ineffective. One way in which
such changed behaviour may be encouraged
is through teacher-to-teacher personal
contact. Rudduck and Kelly found that
attempts to stimulate such interaction
either through teachers' centres or school-
based activities had been made in all six
countries they studied.[5] One problem which
is rarely mentioned in the United Kingdom
literature concerns the mobility of teachers.
If teachers change their jobs frequently,
this might necessitate national standardisa-
tion of practices. Teacher turnover para-
doxically makes for a stable curriculum,
since innovations are often difficult to
initiate without a 'product champion' who
will work enthusiastically to further them.
Keen new teachers may not stay long

enough in a school to become 'insiders'.[6]

According to the Impact and Take-up Project, approximately one-third of teachers had given up using one project or another, and the principal reason given for so doing was that they had changed schools (47%). Other reasons for abandonment of a project were: changes of teaching post (promotion) 18%; judgments of the project's intrinsic worth or lack of it (9%); relative worth in the curriculum (7%); changes in school policy/curriculum (9%).[7]

Another consideration, which is discreetly avoided in the United Kingdom literature, is that of financial incentive. The teacher lacks an economic motive for adopting an innovation. It may be that his promotion prospects will be enhanced by association with recent developments, but on the whole he is paid on the basis of length of service and educational qualifications rather than on his net output, itself very difficult to measure.[8]

Watkins, who ran a number of one-day conferences at Leeds University to introduce school teachers to Schools Council projects, provides from his experiences a number of useful ideas for successful dissemination to teachers.[9] He thought that such conferences had limitations as a dissemination service, because it was unsatisfactory just to present project materials and hope that teachers would absorb project philosophy by some osmotic process. Most projects' aims and objectives are inconsistent with the *status quo*. Moreover, their materials are not usually provided for a clearly defined, already existing school subject. 'Most take a more radical approach, which has evolved over months of team discussion and consultation, and which presents a distinct challenge and alternative to the conventional wisdom in a particular curriculum area.'[10] In other words, the materials do not stand on their own, but are imbued with the educational philosophy of a particular project team, and they should really be considered against the background of that philosophy.

The reason for Watkins' *caveat* is that his experience was that teachers at these conferences wanted to know whether what was offered enabled them to go on teaching as they had always done; if considerable change in their behaviour was required, their interest waned. If teachers simply buy the kit and use it without 'reading the rules', then it is unlikely that they will implement project strategy except by chance. This leads Watkins to argue that some means must be found of creating for teachers who were not involved in the development phase an experience which will enable them to modify their insights in the way in which 'initiates' have already done. To provide for this, future projects should invest in *teacher* development alongside *curriculum* development. He comes very close to describing what might have been done with the HGSS 8-13 Project, when he argues that the aim should be to produce dissemination packages which reproduce in some way the experience of the team in arriving at its conclusions. He agrees with Rudduck and Kelly's proposal that such packages should enable *groups* of teachers to study them, since implementation of curriculum development is a *group* process.

Such dissemination materials will be particularly important where (for example) a school wishes to embark on a project, but the relevant LEA has no policy for local dissemination. In this case, whether the initial enthusiasm of a teacher is converted into action will depend not only on the quality of any induction course, but also on the quality of the teacher's reading and interpretation of project guide books. (His headteacher's support is, of course, essential.)[11]

The Impact and Take-up Project suggested that the decision whether or not to use a project was not so much based, for teachers, upon additional information being available, as much as being a matter of school policy (in primary schools, very much the head-teacher's prerogative).[12]

A similar point can be made with the GYSL project, whose team members rejected the idea that they were simply producing materials. They argued that the materials ensured dissemination, but it was the local groups who ensured implementation.

Such hypotheses are echoed in Shipman's report on the Keele Integrated Studies Project.[13] He found that the persistence of the project's effect on the teachers involved and on their schools was primarily determined by their own input. It did not matter if teachers were critical. As long as they were committed, they would be more likely to produce a lasting impact on their schools. Indeed, dissemination was more likely to be unsuccessful with teachers who simply welcomed or accepted the materials, but did not interact with them in a constructively critical way. The implication of his experience is that, if innovations are to overcome resistance to change, they must not be delivered to teachers like an unopened package. Shipman argues that the successful organisation of planned curriculum changes may depend more on mobilizing teachers into planning and implementation than on getting schools to accept packaged materials. Given the way he thinks teachers plan their lessons, he is pessimistic about how extensive such change can be. He summarises that teachers demand both a detailed plan for action and flexibility to adjust to local school conditions; they ask to be told what to do, only to reject the suggestions as unsuitable for their school.[14] Perhaps innovators have not quite realised the enormous amount of energy and hard work required of the teacher developing new curricular ideas. It was said of the HCP, for example, that: 'The demands on the time and nervous energy of teachers undertaking research and development are considerable and the mental and physical load can be very exhausting, especially if the project is in any way successful. To fail with a project is comparatively easy; to succeed is hard.'[15]

This concern is reflected also in the Schools Council Dissemination Report, which asserts that changes in the curriculum require teachers to be willing to change their ideas, and that some resistance is likely to be encountered. 'The true targets of curriculum innovators are the teachers' knowledge, skill and understanding.' [16] The report argues that although a communication system is essential to dissemination, it is not enough. It will not guarantee the adoption of a project. Curriculum development is justified if it raises school standards by helping teachers to gain self-critical control over what they are doing. Teachers' curricular choice should be expanded, and their critical judgment about what is on offer should be enhanced. Any project will have failed if its ideas are not in the end understood, whether or not the materials are being used.

References

1 Rudduck, J. and Kelly, P., *The Dissemination of Curriculum Development* (NFER, 1976), p.98.
2 Regan, E.M. and Leithwood, K.A., *Effecting Curriculum Change – Experience with the Conceptual Skills Project* (Ontario Institute for Studies in Education, 1974), p.29.
3 Centre of Educational Research and Innovation, *Handbook on Curriculum Development* (OECD, 1975), p.108.
4 Rudduck, J. and Kelly, P., ibid., p.100.
5 ibid., *passim.*
6 Miles, M.B., *Innovation in Education* (New York: Teachers' College, 1964), p.633.
7 Steadman, S.D. *et al., Impact and Take-up Project:* Interim Report (Schools Council Mimeo, 1978), p.104.
8 Miles, M.B., ibid., p.634.
9 Watkins, R., *Curriculum Development and Teacher Development – a Suggestion.* Paper submitted to Schools Council Working Party on Dissemination, 7 November, 1972.
10 ibid., p.2.
11 *Schools Council Working Paper 56:* 'Dissemination of Innovation: The Humanities Curriculum Project' (Evans/Methuen Educational, 1976), p.46.
12 Steadman, S.D. *et al.,* ibid., p.81.
13 Shipman, M.D., 'The Impact of a Curriculum Project', *Curriculum, School and Society,* Taylor, P.H. and Tye, K.A. (eds.) (NFER, 1975), p.211.
14 Shipman, M.D. with Bolam, D. and Jenkins, D., *Inside a Curriculum Project* (Methuen, 1974), p.12.
15 Elliott, J. and MacDonald, B. (eds.), *People in Classrooms.* Occasional Paper No. 2 (Centre for Applied Research in Education, 1975), p.10.
16 *Schools Council Pamphlet 14:* 'Dissemination and In-service Training': Report of the Working Party on Dissemination 1972/3, pp.29-30.

CHAPTER V

THE EVALUATION OF DISSEMINATION

It is difficult to establish testable criteria for evaluating the effectiveness of any particular dissemination strategy. Some projects issue a newsletter for example, but it would be hard to assess whether such items succeed in conveying project philosophy to the uninitiated.[1] Even statistics such as sales figures can be misleading, as shown on page 31.

Just as a curriculum development itself may be evaluated, it is also possible to attempt an assessment of the effectiveness of one type of dissemination strategy. It would presumably be possible to develop criterion-referenced objectives for dissemination, but the same criticisms would apply here as when the method is used to evaluate curriculum development. Similarly, it would also be possible to apply the two main types of objectives-based evaluation, namely formative and summative, to the dissemination process.

Disillusionment with objectives-based systems has grown for a number of reasons. The application of tests is very expensive and time-consuming. Such resources might be allocated more effectively to direct observation in the classroom, and teachers' reports. Often the information gleaned from such tests is tentative, not providing sufficient feedback at either the formative or summative stage to guide decisions about changes to the materials and approach. In the past, evaluation reports have been wrapped up in statistical jargon directed at research workers, rather than presented in language easily understood by the classroom teacher. They have concentrated on whether the project has been a success, rather than on whether an appreciation of it can help teachers' understanding. It would certainly help if project evaluations could be communicated more directly to teachers.[2] Furthermore, it may be that a curriculum development has some effects which were not pre-specified, and which may therefore not be picked out or evaluated by an objective type of assessment. Classroom studies are necessary to complement objective tests, since it cannot be assumed that teachers are using the projects in the way the developers intended.[3] Finally, a classical objectives approach may impede the use of information derived from formative evaluation, since in a controlled experiment it is not possible to redevelop the course in mid-stream.

These problems connected with the objectives approach to evaluation have led to the development of alternative approaches, one of which in particular will be outlined here. This new style of evaluation, which could well be used in the evaluation of dissemination strategies, has been described as 'illuminative' by Parlett and Hamilton.[4]

They summarise their ideas as follows: 'Illuminative evaluation is introduced as belonging to a contrasting "anthropological" research paradigm. Attempted measurement of "educational products" is abandoned for intensive study of the programme as a whole: its rationale and evolution, its operations, achievements and difficulties. The innovation is not examined in isolation, but in the school context or "learning milieu" ... Observation, interviews with participants (students, instructors, administrators and others), questionnaires, and analysis of documents and background information are all combined to help "illuminate" problems, issues and significant programme features.'[5]

Their aims are to investigate how the curriculum development project is being implemented in the schools, and to see what influences affect it. They want to examine what teachers regard as its advantages and disadvantages, and how pupils' intellectual tasks and academic experiences are most affected. They stress that when a project is actually used in a school, it is often modified in various ways, some of them entirely distorting the ideas of the project. So it is very important to investigate within individual schools how a project is being treated.

'In practice, objectives are commonly re-ordered, re-defined, abandoned or forgotten. The original "ideal" formulation ceases to be accurate or, indeed, of much relevance. Few in practice take catalogue descriptions and lists of objectives very seriously, save, it seems, for the traditional evaluator.'[6] In contrast to objective types of evaluation, illuminative evaluation does not necessarily seek to pass judgment on a project for the benefit of feedback to the project team. It seeks more to provide a range of information for a variety of possible readers and users, concentrating on field studies which show the innovation being used in a normal school and describing broadly what happens, and what reactions its users have to it.[7]

For example, according to Hamilton, the evaluation of the Project PHI (Programmed Materials for the Highlands and Islands) incorporated the following data and field-work features: fixed response science attitude and reading tests: a questionnaire survey of audio-visual provision; preliminary site visits to all schools and discussions with other interested parties (e.g. HMIs, administrators); a fixed response teacher questionnaire extending to ten pages; tape recorded interviews with project teachers; participant observation in five schools; comments from teachers at a report-back meeting.[8]

This project showed very clearly the trade-off between different types of evaluation. The creation of carefully validated test instruments may eat into time that could be spent on school visits; or the intensive scrutiny of computer printout may conflict with attempts to provide rapid feedback to sponsors, participants or potential users.[9]

Just as the research designs used for attainment tests vary for many reasons, so there are many types of illuminative evaluation.[10] Its scope, purpose and methods used will depend on many factors: the interests of the body financing the evaluation study; what kind of curriculum development is being evaluated; how many schools, teachers and pupils are involved; how much co-operation and how much access to information are received; what prior experience the researcher has; and how much money is available. These factors apply just as strongly to the evaluation of dissemination as to the evaluation of the curriculum development itself.

Another example of a full-scale 'illuminative' approach is the study of the blind and partially sighted children in ordinary schools entitled *Towards Integration*.[11] The two main features of the researchers' approach were that the study should be geared to the needs of its clients, and that the research design should evolve in the course of study rather than being fixed in advance. The crux of the problem was whether such handicapped children should be educated in normal or special schools. This question divided the professionals sharply. A traditional piece of research would have consisted of a systematic comparative study between the two alternatives, based on tests and questionnaires completed by matched samples of children, the results being subjected to statistical comparison. The aims of this research were, however, quite different. It attempted to bring together a variety of dispersed information; to summarize and portray arguments, opinions, personal and professional convictions developed by those in the schools; and to examine a variety of basic underlying assumptions in the education of such children.[12]

To summarize, evaluation studies are becoming shorter and cheaper, and are reporting more concisely and rapidly. They show a movement away from objective measurement techniques towards more individualistic methods, and are examining what is happening in classrooms rather than inputs and outputs. They are flexibly designed, willing to accept that no simple answers exist.[13]

It is important, however, that evaluation should not move from the extreme of spurious precision to that of arbitrary impressionism. It is true that the traditional method may restrict itself too severely to the measuring of outcomes which can be objectively assessed. But illuminative evaluation may itself suffer from being subjective and unreliable.[14] It may be possible to modify both approaches to make them more useful. The empirical approach may be widened to include unintended as well as pre-specified out-comes. The illuminative approach is developing methods of obtaining information less subjectively. For example, techniques of classroom observation have been devised, using high- or low-inference schedules, video-recording, interaction analysis and so on. Such methods reduce the dependence of the results on the judgment and bias of the observer.

The burden of the above argument is that, because any individual criterion for evaluating dissemination is unlikely to be reliable, it might be more helpful simply to invoke a range of criteria, hoping that by so doing a general impression which is approximately correct will emerge. It is important to have *some* method of discriminating between different approaches to dissemination, so that any findings can be used to determine future policy, thus making dissemination more effective.

The Schools Council Working Party Report suggests five possible approaches.[15] First, the dissemination strategy adopted by a project could be evaluated as it occurred, and altered while still in progress. This form of concurrent evaluation is modelled very much on the 'formative evaluation' of curriculum development itself. Secondly, it may be possible to group projects which have common elements, so that they could all be evaluated together, assuming that dissemination evaluators were appointed to work simultaneously with more than one project. A third approach would be to study particular dissemination techniques, to assess them for the benefit of future projects. For example, the effectiveness of the use of project conferences, the movement of teachers from trial schools, the use of mass media, and the use of teachers' centres could be studied. Fourthly, analytical studies and case histories could be made, based on the established ideas of summative evaluation. A final area of research might investigate such problems as how decisions to adopt innovations are actually taken, what the constraints to exercising 'informed choice' are in practice, and what barriers to implementation exist in schools. To answer some of the questions, both surveys and pure research work may be required.

One plea for such research has come from Harlen, writing about the Science 5-13 Project.[16] She conjectures that, in some three to five years' time, some teachers will be using the project materials, others will have discarded them; some will still not have heard of them, others will have considered but rejected their use. She proceeds to argue that it would be valuable in many ways to inquire into various patterns of usage and non-usage, particularly for the light it would throw on dissemination. For example, how successful had the in-service courses been? Extremely useful data might be obtained for the next wave of curriculum development in science for 5 to 13 year olds. She continues: 'It may be possible, for instance, to distinguish varying degrees in the application of the project's philosophy — from using the units as vehicles for putting the philosophy into practice, to using the units as ideas for teaching in a way quite out of keeping with the philosophy.'[17]

It might be discovered that there are practically no schools in which the project philosophy is being implemented, in which case curriculum developers may have to think again about how realistic their proposals are. On the other hand, it might be found that teachers became more adept at implementing project philosophy as they became more experienced with the materials. It is difficult to see what progress can be made without some evidence of answers to these questions.

The most recent reaction to the afore-mentioned ignorance on the question of the efficacy of dissemination is that the Schools Council has established a project, 'The Impact and Take-up of Schools Council Projects', which with £97,000 hopes to find out what impact their 160 curriculum development projects are making (see Chapter IX).

This chapter concludes with Hamilton's amusing analogy between curriculum innovation and horticulture: 'If a content emphasis can be described as an engineering approach to curriculum development, then the situational emphasis is much closer to gardening. Curricula are devised according to soil type, and then close attention is paid to preparing the ground. Given this thought, the seeding is a routine affair soon overshadowed by a programme of careful but unobstrusive nurturing.

'In theoretical terms, the assessment of curricula with a situational emphasis is extremely difficult. A short-term index of success might be the germination of the seeds but, ultimately, a set of long-term goals is the overriding concern. These goals might include the production of more autonomous citizens, the development of self-supporting teachers' centres, or the eradication of pupil alienation. In the absence of short-term goals or behavioural objectives, the criterion problem is severe. Even when criteria can be provided, they cannot be regarded as absolute since by the terms of the curriculum emphasis different situations will promote different levels of outcome. If it can be measured at all, the success of such criteria is more likely to be based on the subjective quality of the flowers than upon the objective weight of the fruits.'[18]

28

References

1 *Schools Council Pamphlet 14:* 'Dissemination and In-service Training': Report of the Working Party on Dissemination 1972/3.
2 Stenhouse, L., *An Introduction to Curriculum Research and Development* (Heinemann Educational, 1975), p.106.
3 Hamilton, D., *Curriculum Evaluation* (Open Books, 1976), p.28.
4 Parlett, M. and Hamilton, D., *Evaluation as Illumination: a new approach to the study of innovating programmes.* Occasional paper of the Centre for Research in the Educational Sciences, University of Edinburgh (unpublished Mimeo, October 1972), p.1.
5 ibid., *passim.*
6 Parlett, M. and Hamilton, D., 'Evaluation by Illumination', *Curriculum Evaluation Today: Trends and Implications,* Tawney, D. (ed.), Schools Council Research Studies (Macmillan, 1976), p.90.
7 Hamilton, D., ibid., p.38.
8 ibid., p.59.
9 ibid., p.62.
10 See note 6 above, p.92.
11 Jamieson, M., Parlett, M. and Pocklington, K., *Towards Integration. A study of blind and partially sighted children in ordinary schools* (NFER, 1977), *passim.*
12 ibid., p.19.
13 Hamilton, D., ibid., p.70.
14 Harlen, W., 'Change and development in evaluation strategy', ibid., Tawney, D. (ed.), p.31.
15 See note 1 above, pp.25-6.
16 Harlen, W., *Science 5-13: A Formative Evaluation* (Macmillan, 1975).
17 ibid., p.90.
18 Hamilton, D., ibid., p.78.

CHAPTER VI

THE DISSEMINATION OF THE
HISTORY, GEOGRAPHY AND SOCIAL
SCIENCE 8-13 PROJECT

The analysis in the foregoing chapters has raised a number of questions about dissemination policy which will be applied in a detailed analysis of the HGSS 8-13 Project (henceforward referred to as 'the project').

The first question to be considered is whether the project followed a policy of positive promotion of its ideas and materials. In this case, it would be appropriate to distinguish between its policy towards ideas and materials. The former it did seek to proselytize, but the materials were not actively promoted by the project, in the sense of finished products to be bought and used.

The project's attitude towards dissemination was strongly influenced by the 'movement' model discussed earlier. The team likened an initiative's development to ripples on a pool when the waters are disturbed by a stone. However, there is rarely only one stone, and one set of ripples; rather a series of related ideas are diffused which, in the case of a project, can be taken up and reformulated as a recognisable whole.[1] Such an analogy described the project's philosophy much more accurately than the 'centre-periphery' model, in which ideas are spread by controlled dissemination from a centre and absorbed at the periphery. Rather, the project intended teachers, individually and in groups, to maintain innovation in schools.

They felt that their methods followed the usual way in which developments in education actually take place. 'The project team has produced publications, made contacts in a few areas, watched to see in detail how these developed, and for the rest, left its ideas and other similar ideas to grow and spread.'[2] However, the disadvantage of this pattern of dissemination (fully realized by the project team themselves) was that the project attracted less publicity than those espousing the 'centre-periphery' model. The strategy had greater risks than centrally controlled dissemination, because the project's ideas might be altered or lost without trace as the 'movement' developed. It would not have regarded the former outcome as a total disaster. Indeed, it took pains to stress that it did not seek to hand down a message 'in the hope that it will be lovingly transcribed from generation to generation.'[3] It aimed much more to stimulate a process which, though unpredictable, would be responsible, effective and self-sustaining. It would have regarded success as being attained when the project was superseded by the process of development which it had set in motion. Doubts must be expressed however about the publicity policy of the project when it is agreed by the Team themselves that even within the project's pilot schools, there were members of staff who were only dimly, if at all, aware of the project's existence.[4]

The project materials can be divided into four main categories. First there is a book[5] which is a basic statement of the project's point of view. This forms an important element in the dissemination strategy. It contains practical advice to teachers, and it could act as a useful discussion document for teachers forming a group in a teachers' centre or elsewhere. It also serves to advise all those interested in the education world about the philosophy and methods of the project.

However, one caveat must be entered here. The project team stressed that they designed their other publications on the assumption that they would be considered in conjunction with this basic book.[6] But such an assumption is unrealistic; the book is expensive and 'theoretical', and teachers' scarce resources are much more likely to be allocated to the units themselves* (see Chapter VIII and Appendix II). However, this book was reprinted two years after publication, so presumably sales have been quite buoyant.

This leads on to consideration of the fifteen units and their role in dissemination. Their purpose is to serve as examplars, showing how the project's ideas might be worked out in practice. Of particular relevance to dissemination are the unit guides, addressed to teachers, which indicate how the themes are based on objectives and key concepts and suggest how the various components of the published units might be used.

The third document, entitled *Themes in Outline* (published in 1977, at £3.25 for 64 pages), is intended to help teachers to design units for themselves on other themes.[7] Here again, the team stressed that the outlines

were intended to help the teacher to make some units for himself, but like the published units themselves, did not and were not intended to constitute a course. It may be, however, that such outlines will be used prescriptively, whatever the team might wish.

The fourth type of publication consists of a series of support booklets, on such topics as 'Games and Simulations in the Classroom', 'Teaching for Concepts' and 'Using Sources and Resources'.[8] This series was intended to give particular help to teachers on aspects of the project's work which, during the schools programme and the dissemination phase, repeatedly appeared important, yet for which many teachers did not feel adequately equipped. Each of these booklets is some 30 to 50 pages in length, and all cost more than £1. In the writer's view, it is very unlikely that teachers will buy such costly documents. Tony Howarth states (in *TES* 3.12.76, p.43): 'If the project set out its aims and objectives at length, it seems to have paid scant attention to the procedures of that market place in which curriculum development is what you can afford in money and time, not what may be merely desirable.' If this is true, then unless the project's philosophy is encapsulated in the units themselves, it simply will not be perpetuated. Although it may be true that 'these publications constitute a substantial array of pedagogic equipment'[9], they will not be of much use if they do not reach the teachers.

It is possible to provide some information about sales of Project publications, but care must be taken in interpreting these figures, for reasons already stated. Table 2 opposite gives sales figures up to August 1976, just for the Money Unit. The Inspection Copy material, which was provided freely, consisted of one copy of a booklet: 'Every-

* For example, Tony Howarth, in a review of the project's materials (TES 3.12.76, p.43), wrote: 'commentary on Bloom's *Taxonomy of Educational Objectives* is not appropriate for most middle school teachers. Similarly, Bernstein, Bruner *et al.* are not important in themselves; they only become important when their ideas are relayed in ways which will make teachers sit up and take notice.'

day Life in Tikopea', a Teachers' Guide and four sample run-off sheets of the spirit-masters.

Table 2: Sales of the Money Unit (up to August, 1976) (Figures supplied by the publishers)	
Inspection Copy Material (provided *gratis)*	
Primary Schools	161
Secondary Schools	34
Advisers/Inspectors	18
Teachers' Centres	23
Colleges of Education	35
	271
Complete Units Purchased (£10 each)	
Primary Schools	4
Secondary Schools	6
Advisers/Inspectors/LEAs	17
Teachers' Centres	18
Colleges of Education (+ University Depts. of education)	25
Miscellaneous	6
	76

As can readily be seen, the figure of inspection copy material distributed far exceeds that of complete units purchased, and it could be maintained that the publishers were far too generous with it. Teachers might be able to operate the unit on the basis of the inspection copy material alone. An important corollary of this would be that if they did so, they would be using the unit without even the 'Place, Time and Society'[10] introductory booklet to explain project philosophy. The Money Unit was put on the market in September, 1975, as one of the first units of the project to be published. Indeed, by December, 1976, only 6 out of the 15 planned units had been published, and it is remarkable that within one year (according to the publishers) only 10 schools in the entire United Kingdom had bought the unit. Chapter IX investigates all these schools, to ascertain what happened to the unit after it had been bought by the schools or other agencies.

It was not possible to obtain figures for the sales of other project units, though the publishers admit that they have been modest. It may be that sales of the Money Unit were so low because a primary or middle school's allocation for social studies would normally receive low priority, although this appears to be improving: 'here and there, schools and LEAs have begun to recognise that Place, Time and Society deserve a larger share of the available resources and support than has often been their lot. For too long they have had to take their place at the end of the queue for equipment, materials and technical assistance, and to accept, especially in secondary schools, the crumbs of the time-table left over after the claims of others have been staked.'[11] Another possibility is that, given the very small number of primary and middle school teachers with any kind of background in Economics (as stated earlier, only 3-4% have social science training), the target teachers may well have opted for those units which better complemented their geographical or historical training.

A final publication of this project was a termly newsletter, sent freely to all interested parties and project schools, which provided a regular flow of information about the project. By the end of 1972, 1000 people were receiving it.[12]

Any strictures made about the project should not be interpreted as criticisms of the project team. After all, they aimed to stimulate local groups of teachers to prepare materials for their own use based on a general framework of objectives and key concepts but taking into account their own unique position. According to the most recent publication about the project,[13] the project team were very much constrained by the Schools Council Publications Department. This department allowed publishers to use the Schools Council imprimatur in exchange for the assurance that the project materials were fully developed and ready for use in schools.

However, the HGSS 8-13 Project team regarded their most important publication as being the handbook on curriculum planning and the short teacher support booklets. For them, the units were only ancillary, and it was hoped that the former would achieve far more sales than the latter. But the publishers expected very sophisticated packaged kits, and some of the project team probably felt unable to spend more time and effort on the units than they had planned to do. This seriously detracted from the resources they could devote to the dissemination phase.[14]

The next group of questions to consider about the dissemination of the project concern whether it involved the teacher adopting a new role, and if so, what provision was made by the project for bringing about such a change. The most important innovation in this project was the idea that the teachers were provided with a conceptual framework of objectives and key concepts, but were intended to develop their own programmes, not necessarily based on the team's output. But in fact teachers have very little time for such work. Also, the team themselves realised that teachers who had not had any sort of formal apprenticeship in the social disciplines might well be worried about what was involved in using those disciplines as resources. Repeatedly, during the pilot phase and later in the dissemination period, teachers complained to the Team that they had no time for adequate curriculum planning.[15] This reaction caused the Team to suggest that there should be regular, and officially supported, provision within a school's programme for teachers to have time to plan and to produce materials. Furthermore, they argued that it should be possible to encourage more two-way communication between the teachers of older and younger pupils, particularly across the primary/secondary divide. But like so many of the project team's hortatory remarks, no machinery is suggested for effecting such a change in the present contractionary financial climate. Such remarks are epitomized in the frequent intonation in project publications, that 'the units are in a sense crutches, to be discarded in the course when the process of thinking deeply, systematically and reflectively about curriculum planning has reached a stage at which this abandonment becomes justified.'[16]

The project team did gain some experience in gauging teachers' reactions when the project was presented to them. They seemed to pass through three stages. First, they were concerned to learn about the use of objectives, key concepts, and subject disciplines as resources. At this stage, they only made slight changes to the content of what they were teaching. Gradually, as they became more familiar with the project's objectives and key concepts, they began to apply them more fully and extensively, and with growing confidence, in planning their pupils' curriculum. Finally, they began to adapt the objectives and key concepts to their own needs, building up units and data banks. However, as far as can be discovered, it seems that the teachers who went through these stages were those who were intimately connected with the project, either in the pilot or early dissemination stages. It would be unlikely that the reactions of teachers 'outside' the project would follow the same developments. It may be that such teachers would not progress beyond the first stage.

Such a prediction is lent weight by the experience of the Schools Council *Progress in Learning Science* Project research team.[17] Each of the various new curricula in science had its own philosophy to be found in a statement of its aims. But they had in common a desire to move away from teaching science as a set body of knowledge, received facts and opinions, and encourage more pupil participation in exploring new ideas. But over a quarter of the teachers in the survey never encouraged the designing of experiments through their questioning, and there were both chemistry and physics teachers who never asked questions on what pupils observed during practical work. Yet these were just the type of activities expected to take place with the approach characterised in the Nuffield Science programme. This research team's findings suggested then that there was considerable dissonance between the curriculum developers' aims and the related practice in the classroom.

'In retrospect, therefore, we cannot carry out successful development aimed at altering styles of teaching as well as content from a far away position remote from the classroom. The curriculum model used in STEP in which the developer acts as co-ordinator and editor of materials prepared and tested by local groups of teachers, would appear to be more appropriate. But it is essential that the initial use of these materials must be carefully monitored, using interaction analysis techniques.'[18]

The next question to consider is whether the project team differentiated between the groups which it attempted to influence, and whether they worked out what each group required, and provided the requisite information, involvement and materials. This question may be applied either to the dissemination phase (during the project's lifetime) or to the diffusion phase after the project had ended, and connected with it are the related questions of whether the team transferred responsibility for dissemination to some other body, and whether they organised a continuing training programme and local support systems in teachers' centres or elsewhere.

The published information about the project does not provide enough evidence to answer the question about discrimination between different groups. Certainly the team were aware that different sections of the educational world had different needs to be appealed to in different ways. For example, in setting up in-service training, they began to evolve second-order objectives — not just for the pupils or teachers — but objectives for teacher-educators too. The team came to appreciate the role that would have to be played by key figures in the educational world in maintaining the project's momentum after their dissolution. They ranked among such key figures as administrators, college, university and polytechnic staffs, HMIs, advisors, teachers' centre and professional centre workers, publishers and teachers.[19] They considered that perhaps the most important issue to emerge from the project's dissemination trials, from the administrator's point of view, was the question of responsibility for maintaining the momentum of the project itself. Their conclusion was somewhat astringent: 'If there is no central machinery impelling a local organisation to sustain the impetus of an innovation, then either some effective substitute must be found, or the innovation will wither. Someone has to act as a *sponsor* for the project and its sequel. He in his turn will depend for his effectiveness on the initiative and impact of intermediate level "co-ordinators".'[20] Perhaps with hindsight the team were suggesting that rather more positive promotion of their ideas might have been desirable. In retrospect, the Deputy Director of the project felt that the limited success of the dissemination phase could partly be accounted for by the multiplicity of its reference groups. It is possible that too much emphasis was placed on middle and secondary schools, and that a significant reference group, the primary school, was not fully involved. Moreover, although history and geography teachers had their professional bodies and advisers, the social studies approach had few protagonists. The former groups had often been brought together by interest in other projects in their fields, whilst those teachers interested in social studies had no organising apparatus.[21]

The team had started its dissemination programme in 1973. At that stage, teachers and LEAs were approached to find out what would be the most effective means of establishing a continuing process of curriculum-planning after the project had ended. For a start, the project had to ensure its continuance in those schools and LEAs in which the experimental programme itself had been conducted. These areas are shown in Table 3 [22] (see page 36). They do seem unduly dispersed throughout the UK, given the Liverpool base of the project team. It also launched a limited number of new initiatives in different types of area. However, the task appeared to be beset with more problems than had been anticipated: 'The outcome of this led to a modification of the Team's original ideas and to a realistic appraisal of what is practicable.'[23]

The team's dissemination strategy consisted primarily of a series of workshops, both in familiar and new areas, in which teachers would come together and formulate schemes and develop materials of their own.[24] For this, the project needed to ensure that adequate support and facilities were available in particular places. According to the project profile issued by the Schools Council, the dissemination programme would be carefully evaluated and was intended to throw light on questions of curriculum development in general.[25] This profile added the information that the new areas would number six. But no such evaluation report has been published. The dissemination programme planned in 1973 was an attenuated version of that first put forward in 1972. The constraints of time, finance and what was practicable were already imposing themselves. In 1972 it had been hoped that there would be workshops in teachers' centres, colleges of education, University Schools of Education and in some instances inside individual large schools, to put the project's strategy into effect and to extend, adapt and amend it.[26]

By 1975, the pattern which emerged had become clearer. As stated on page 10, there were five types of area in which the project had planned their dissemination programme:

'1. within the existing trial schools to colleagues of the trial teachers; 2. within the trial areas to neighbouring schools, using trial school teachers in the workshops; 3. in a number of new areas where the project team organised workshops; 4. in new areas where local co-ordinators, after attending an induction course, would organise workshops supported by the project team; 5. developing a system of contacts through which information on the project could be broadcast so that groups and individuals are aware who else in their area is working on similar lines, leading perhaps to the formation of further workshops'.[27]

Without a very extensive and costly research programme,* it would not be possible to find out how closely the actual activity across the country conformed to this pattern. Martin's centre at Purbeck fitted somewhere between styles 4 and 5. Activity developed as a result of his interest in gathering local resources for the middle years of schooling, to serve newly created middle schools in the area. Teachers in the area had told him that they needed guidance in the social studies area. In 1973, Martin attended an induction course and returned to Purbeck to set up workshops. In 1974, heads of eleven local schools came to the teachers' centre to discuss and examine the project. Some of the project team visited the centre, and groups were formed to plan work units. Some schools worked independently, but four joined together and formed 'the Swanage Group'. This group held extra meetings, to thrash out the work units and possible sharing of resources. Day meetings continued at the centre at half-termly intervals to report on progress and exchange ideas and problems.

* See Appendix I for an account of the findings of the Impact and Take-up Project with respect to the HGSS 8-13 Project.

The teachers involved with the project reacted favourably to the work in their reports, and according to Martin, produced exciting examples of children's work. As a result of requests from other centre leaders in Dorset, and the feeling of the group that other teachers in the Purbeck area should be involved, Martin decided to organise a county dissemination conference for the project to be followed by the initiation of workshops in other centres in Dorset by the Purbeck team of teachers.

Presumably the project team would have regarded the kind of development outlined above as an example of the good practice which they were attempting to foster. The initiation of the whole local development depended on the enthusiasm of the local teachers' centre warden. It could be regarded as unsatisfactory to base dissemination policy on the hope that sufficient key figures will display such enthusiasm and organisational powers.

Martin too is sceptical about whether workshops would proliferate without a more structured organisation, with its implication of financial support and encouragement of teacher release for in-service training.[28] He wonders who will provide the driving force to create new workshops, and whether workshops will continue after initial work units have been produced. Such group workshops are particularly important for primary school teachers (for whom, however, release is more difficult) who on the whole are comparatively isolated (in their teaching of social studies), and who therefore need to be involved with teachers from other schools to facilitate mutual support and exchange of ideas. Nevertheless, the experience in Purbeck was that, although planning was co-operative, the teachers failed to contribute resources from their own work units, telling the warden that

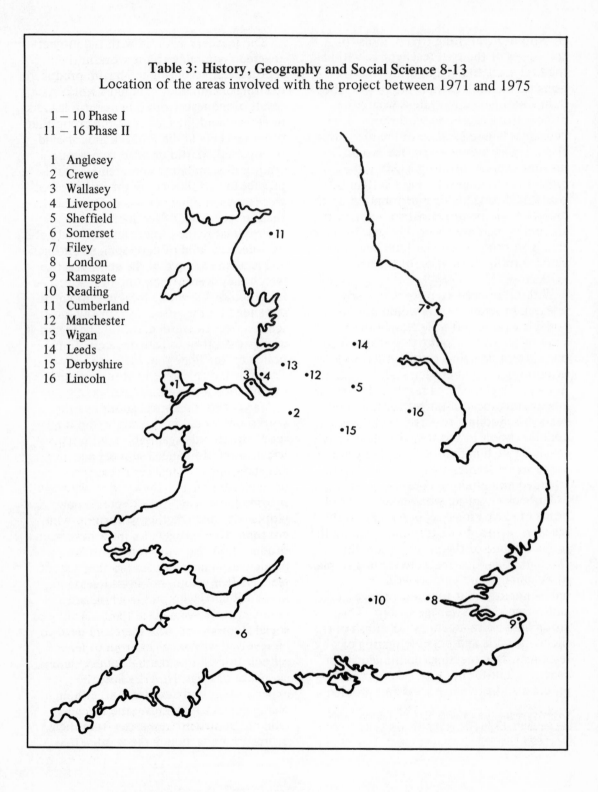

Table 3: History, Geography and Social Science 8-13
Location of the areas involved with the project between 1971 and 1975

1 – 10 Phase I
11 – 16 Phase II

1   Anglesey
2   Crewe
3   Wallasey
4   Liverpool
5   Sheffield
6   Somerset
7   Filey
8   London
9   Ramsgate
10   Reading
11   Cumberland
12   Manchester
13   Wigan
14   Leeds
15   Derbyshire
16   Lincoln

they preferred to keep some things up their sleeves rather than pool everything. Here is an example of how teachers' attitudes themselves would need to be changed in order for project dissemination philosophy to be fully implemented.

Before attempting an overall assessment of the dissemination of the project, there are a number of other questions to consider which are prompted by the discussion in Chapter III. The Schools Council Report on Dissemination[29] suggested that a well-organised network of teachers' group leaders should be established to maintain two-way communication between teachers and the project. The only published information on this desideratum states that the project team established working groups of teachers in about twenty LEAs in England and Wales. It should be noted that it could not be stated, after the end of the project, in precisely how many LEAs it had been operating.[30] It was hoped that these groups, with teachers, teachers' centre wardens, college of education tutors and advisers working together, would maintain local initiatives long after the end of the project in August, 1975. Unfortunately, nothing is known about what happened to these teachers' groups in the long run.

The project did not appoint liaison officers, but the Schools Council team of Field Officers had a disseminating function, although this project was only one amongst many which they handled.

As already stated, a 'Project Profile' was available for any interested party, but no distribution figures have been published for this document. Apart from the booklets mentioned earlier when discussing publications, the project produced no 'training materials' of the type to be suggested in Chapter VII. The project did not receive any publicity through coverage in any radio, television, or Open University programmes. As far as is known, few attempts were made by the team to build contacts with the media, but, according to the Impact and Take-up Project, connections *were* made between the project and the BBC Schools TV series 'Scan' and 'Near and Far'.

The final question to be asked is how successful the project has been, in terms of teachers being able to understand its ideas and materials sufficiently well for them to be able to use them in school if they wish to do so. So far as the Money Unit is concerned, some attempt was made by the authors to explain certain economic concepts for the benefit of the teachers of the unit, and suggestions for further reading are given. It was in fact one of the project's aims to try to provide some help for teachers when they wanted to learn more for themselves about the social disciplines.[31] The team stated that in each of the published units, the material was written and structured in such a way that the contribution of the disciplines became clear in the teacher's guide to the unit. On the question of whether teachers understand project ideas, it will become evident from the next chapter that the writer takes the view that it is possible and indeed probable that teachers will 'take' the materials and 'by-pass' the project philosophy, unless (which is not the case here) the materials themselves are integrated with that philosophy. This view is reinforced by the conclusions of the *Progress in Learning Science* Project referred to above,[32] namely that while some of the limitations to the transmission of project aims arose from lack of resources and technical assistance in schools, study of classroom processes suggested that early developers failed to take into account the consistency of the teacher's approach, irrespective of content change.

The project itself made the following prognosis of the outcome of its work. The experience of the team in monitoring the dissemination programme suggested that total transformation or oblivion were unlikely. The actual outcome might well be a patchwork across the country, in which some places were more closely involved than others in curriculum planning for the social subjects in the middle years of schooling. Some would show much more direct influence from the project than others. They would not regard such an uneven distribution as unsatisfactory, provided that it arose from the 'deep, systematic and reflective thinking' on which the project laid its greatest emphasis. They argued that that would be genuine curriculum planning, for its growing points would be in the schools themselves. Chapter VIII assesses how closely this prediction is borne out by the pattern of activity across the country.

Finally, it appears that the suggestion reported in Chapter III, that the Schools Council felt that the HGSS 8-13 Project might still benefit from a dissemination phase, has borne fruit. It was announced in the September 1978 Newsletter of the Schools Council that £41,563 had been granted to provide a National Co-ordinator for three years from September 1978, to be based like the original project at the University of Liverpool School of Education.

The task of the National Co-ordinator is to re-establish contact with existing project networks within LEAs, subject associations and other professional bodies; to develop systematic links with Schools Council Dissemination Centres, all LEAs in England and Wales where no contact at present exists, and Colleges of Higher Education and other teacher education agencies; and to encourage and support in-service and pre-service education in the teaching of the social subjects.

Other objectives of the new phase include the development of ideas on assessment in the social subjects and on continuity in learning.[33]

References

1 Schools Council History, Geography and Social Science 8-13 Project: *Curriculum Planning in History, Geography and Social Science,* by the Research Team (Collins, 1976), p.162.
2 ibid., p.153.
3 Blyth, W.A.L. *et al., Place, Time and Society 8-13: An Introduction* (Collins, 1975), p.31.
4 See note 1 above, p.159.
5 See note 1 above.
6 Blyth, W.A.L. *et al.,* ibid., p.28.
7 Derricott, R. *et al., Themes in Outline,* Schools Council (Collins, 1977).
8 Published by Collins for the Schools Council.
9 Blyth, W.A.L. *et al.,* ibid., p.30.
10 ibid., p.31.
11 ibid., p.7.
12 Blyth, W.A.L. *et al.,* Schools Council History, Geography and Social Science 8-13 Project: *An Interim Statement* (Schools Council, September 1972), p.1.
13 Blyth, W.A.L. *et al.,* 'Aspects of power in the genesis and development of one curriculum project' in *Power in the Curriculum: Issues in Curriculum Studies,* Richards, C. (ed.) (Nafferton, 1978), pp.149-162.
14 ibid., p.158.
15 See note 1 above, p.156.
16 See note 1 above, p.109.
17 Eggleston, J.F., Galton, M.J. and Jones, M.E., *Processes and Products of Science Teaching,* Schools Council Research Studies (Macmillan, 1976), pp.121-2.
18 ibid., p.122.
19 Blyth, W.A.L., 'One Development Projects' Awkward Thinking about Objectives' in *Journal of Curriculum Studies,* Vol.6 No.2, November 1974, p.101.
20 See note 1 above, pp.173-4.
21 Derricott, R., 'The HGSS Project: a phoenix in the middle years' in *The Social Science Teacher,* Vol.8 No.1, October 1978, pp.18-21.
22 Schools Council, 'Achieving Implementation of Projects: Some conclusions from growing experience of dissemination and teacher support programmes, and some implications', unpublished paper.
23 See note 1 above, p.19.
24 Blyth, W.A.L., Schools Council History, Geography and Social Science 8-13 Project: *Spotlights, a Summary of the Project's Approach* (unpublished Mimeo, 1973), p.37.
25 Schools Council History, Geography and Social Science 8-13 (HU 08 03) Project Profile (July 1973), p.27.
26 See note 12 above, p.21.
27 Martin, K.A., *Patterns of Dissemination: A Tale of Two Projects* (unpublished Mimeo, June 1975), p.16.
28 ibid., p.20.
29 *Schools Council Pamphlet 14:* 'Dissemination and In-service Training': Report of the Working Party on Dissemination 1972/3.
30 Derricott, R., 'Place, Time and Society 8-13' in *Dialogue,* No.21, Autumn 1975, pp.8-9.
31 See note 1 above, p.35.
32 See note 17 above.
33 See note 21 above, p.21.

CHAPTER VII

DIFFUSION THROUGH PACKAGED
KITS

The practice of attempting to encapsulate a
curriculum development project's work in
the form of a materials kit is typical of
many national projects, such as the
Humanities Curriculum Project. In the
absence of means for effecting aftercare,
such kits bear the full responsibility for
post-project diffusion. This chapter
considers in detail the Money Unit,
produced by the History, Geography and
Social Science 8-13 Project, as a vehicle for
the diffusion of the project's ideas.

In order to decide whether the Money
Unit adequately reflects project philosophy,
it is necessary to explain at some length
what that philosophy appears to be. Then
the unit is evaluated in the context of the
primary school classroom.

1. Does the Money Unit adequately reflect the project's philosophy?

It is necessary to differentiate between the
concepts of reflection and of transmission
of project philosophy. Unless there are no
major discrepancies between project
philosophy, as explained in project
publications, and the ideas incorporated in
the unit, the question of the unit's
effectiveness as proselytizer is an academic
one.

A. What **Was** *Project Philosophy?*
In order to resolve this problem, evidence
of project philosophy must be sought. This
is a difficult task because of the diffuse

nature of the project and because project
thinking developed during the lifetime of
the project. Team members acknowledged
this in *Curriculum Planning* ...[1]

The Research Team's approach to
curriculum planning started from the
premise that the continuing development
of the curriculum must depend on the
launching, within each unique situation, of
a process of curriculum planning which
would include the establishment of aims,
the development of programmes of work
(or syllabuses), and the making of
appropriate materials.[2] Emphasis was placed
on the *process* of curriculum development
rather than on the development of materials.
Three values were to be borne in mind
during this process. Ethnocentricity should
be avoided, children should be exposed to
problems rather than shielded from them,
and children's autonomy should be
developed through teacher autonomy.
Teachers were not expected to be social
science experts, but *mediators,* with
sufficient knowledge to draw upon the
disciplines.[3]

The team encouraged teachers to think
about aims, derive objectives from those
aims, using key concepts as a means of
drawing upon subject disciplines as
resources, and developing themes into units
by procedures through which the objectives
could be effectively pursued. Their central
recommendation, however, was that
teachers should think deeply, systematically,
and reflectively about themes and units and
all aspects of their teaching, that they

should work together to evolve a more purposeful curriculum in the social subjects, and that they should develop the materials needed to implement it in their unique situations.[4]

The team put forward a classification of objectives based on two main categories: intellectual, social and physical skills; and values, attitudes, interests (see Table 4).

All of these objectives are intended to be jointly pursued throughout the years 8-13.

The object is to ensure that the Table is brought into play, to ensure that over a period of time and in the design of a sequence of units, no one set of objectives is unduly neglected.[5]

It is important to note that the main function of the 'key concepts' is to enable *teachers* to see subject matter from a new and more co-ordinated standpoint. The key concepts suggested are: Communication, Power, Values and Beliefs, Conflict and

Table 4. Classification of Objectives for HGSS 8-13 Project

SKILLS			PERSONAL QUALITIES
Intellectual	Social	Physical	Interests, Attitudes, Values
1. The ability to find information from a variety of sources, in a variety of ways.	1. The ability to participate within small groups.	1. The ability to manipulate equipment.	1. The fostering of curiosity through the encouragement of questions.
2. The ability to communicate findings through an appropriate medium.	2. An awareness of significant groups within the community and the wider society.	2. The ability to manipulate equipment to find and communicate information.	2. The fostering of a wariness of over-commitment to one framework of explanation and the possible distortion of facts and the omission of evidence.
3. The ability to interpret pictures, charts, graphs, maps, etc.	3. A developing understanding of how indivuals relate to such groups.	3. The ability to explore the expressive powers of the human body to communicate ideas and feelings.	
4. The ability to evaluate information.	4. A willingness to consider participating constructively in the activities associated with these groups.	4. The ability to plan and execute expressive activities to communicate ideas and feelings.	3. The fostering of a willingness to explore personal attitudes and values to relate these to other people's.
5. The ability to organise information through concepts and generalisations.	5. The ability to exercise empathy (i.e. the capacity to imagine accurately what it might be like to be someone else).		4. The encouraging of an openness to the possibility of change in attitudes and values.
6. The ability to formulate and test hypotheses and generalisations.			5. The encouragement of worthwhile and developing interests in human affairs.

Consensus, Continuity and Change, Similarity and Difference, Causes and Consequences. The team stressed however that there was nothing sacrosanct about their original seven.

Finally, the team's aim in publishing the kits of materials was that they should serve as examples, temporary guides, until teachers build up for themselves something more permanent. They suggested that, like their Table of Objectives and Key Concepts, the units should be adapted by teachers to their unique situation.[6]

The question concerning the criteria and methods adopted by the Project Team for the selection of their 'key concepts' is problematic. According to the *Interim Statement,* 'the list of seven key concepts was drawn up by agreement within the team and with the teachers in the trial schools.'[7] A philosophical critique points out that the project offers no formal list of criteria for the selection of the seven key concepts.[8] Secondly, the list was apparently drawn up without consultation with 'content specialists'. However, this ignores the fact that the team members themselves were subject specialists. At the beginning of the project, in 1971, the team was impressed with the necessity for a conceptual approach. The members were encouraged by their steering committee to decide which concepts were central to the disciplines and whether they could build up a logical hierarchy through which they could sequence the work. They drew up a list of the key concepts in their various disciplines. They then looked at their lists and tried to pick out concepts which were common to the disciplines involved. This is how they came to settle on the seven key concepts, which were interdisciplinary in that all the Project Team felt their subjects could contribute.

The Project Team repeatedly took pains to stress that the objectives, key concepts and kits of materials themselves were not prescriptive. They saw the units as resources for teacher education rather than resources for children to be used from A to Z, so that if the teachers elaborated or pruned them, that is the way that they intended them to be used. If teachers did not want to use these key concepts, it did not matter. So long as they had some strong co-ordinating ideas in their course, it was not so important what they were.

Such ideas provoke the criticism that rational curriculum planning, which requires clear descriptions of rules and criteria, is impossible and will inevitably be replaced by the exercise of intuition. As Kingdom points out: 'If we take seriously the project's remark that their choice of seven key concepts is "arbitrary, but not irresponsible", its injunction that teachers should develop their own lists of key concepts is an encouragement to teachers to make arbitrary choices, that is, choices made without the benefit of rational bases for choosing.'[9]

In the *Interim Statement,* it is made reasonably clear that the main function of the key concepts is in the selection of content.[10] Kingdom shows how in practice the process of curriculum development worked rather differently. In a section describing the development of a teaching unit in a trial school, it is said that: 'One of the sessions allowed for forward planning of the first units, and with objectives and key concepts fresh in their minds the teachers began structuring a unit entitled "I do like to be beside the sea-side". They had come to the conference with this idea already formed.' This idea for the unit was chosen, before the conference, for three reasons: it had 'social history potential', it was of 'inherent interest to pupils living at a sea-side resort', and it was likely that resources for teaching would be readily available. Kingdom opines that the teachers' initial selection of content had been made on the basis of some prior conception of the suitability of certain material for a social history project, on the basis of predicted student interest, and on the basis of convenience. Their initial selection of content was, therefore made independently of the use of any key concepts. If the team thought that procedure legitimate, it would follow that the determination of curriculum content in the project is based on criteria other than that of the use of key concepts, including if not the intuitive then certainly the unarticulated preconceptions of individual teachers as to the suitability of material. Kingdom proceeds to make the strong point that on such a view, most of the project's work on content selection is redundant, and the 'rehabilitation of content' in curriculum planning requires other sponsors. If, however, the team thought the procedure illegitimate, the onus would be on it to ensure that key concepts *did* determine content in any future procedures for the production of teaching units.[11] As will be shown below, very few safeguards of this nature were inserted into the Money Unit.

A further difficulty with the key concepts is that they are so general as to make it very difficult to exclude content on the ground of irrelevance. If they are intended as a filter for curriculum content, then they need to be operational. The impracticality of key concepts as criteria for the selection of subject matter leads Kingdom to suggest that this is perhaps why some teachers are attracted to highly specific curriculum proposals and to accompanying syllabuses, why they are not insulted by attempts at 'teacher-proof' curricula, and why on the contrary they are prepared to give up the idea of free choice

of curriculum content when that is no more than an opportunity for the exercise of intuition and for the inclusion of the teacher's pet topics.[12]

No stress is laid by the project on any kind of developmental approach to the teaching of History, Geography and Social Science to the 8-13 age range. There is almost no consideration of Bruner's spiral curriculum concept, and Piagetian theory is largely ignored. It is stated that the children are one of the four basic variables, along with teachers, schools and environments, which must be borne in mind when devising the curriculum, and which constrain what can be done. Some of the skills which pupils are meant to acquire from the project are quite sophisticated. During the schools trials, teachers put before children hypotheses and generalisations to be tested, in the hope that these would be understood for what they were and that, in due course, children would come to set up their own hypotheses and test their own generalisations, being ready to reconsider them when contrary instances were found. This is the sort of thinking which Piaget places in his most sophisticated category of 'formal operations' and, since it has become common to regard this as a property of adolescence, it may appear strange that the project should seem to disregard the conventional wisdom of the day by placing emphasis on thinking of this kind in the middle years of schooling. However, Blyth asserts that this is deliberate. It is not assumed that children of eight can do it except in very specific instances; this is one of the ways in which progression in learning in the 8-13 age range has to be systematically considered. The Project Team considered that children are potentially able to start this sort of thinking sooner than some people have thought, or perhaps wished. The project believed that children should be helped to come to terms with their accelerated intellectual growth, not shielded from it. 'What is more, this is true of the less able and less privileged children too. They have their modes of thinking which mature irrespective of schooling, and if the school excludes these modes from its operations, then they will use those modes to exclude its operations from their notion of reality.'[13] It will be seen below that this lack of specific guidelines with respect to the sequencing of concept development in the Money Unit caused some problems.

B. Did the Money Unit incorporate Project Philosophy?

Having explored the main issues relating to adoption of the project's curriculum strategy, the actual Money Unit must now be tested against these criteria to assess its adequacy as a reflector of project ideas. Since the project team ignored the question of structure, the unit's use of the derivation/ articulation approach rather than a 'spiral' approach did not contravene project aims. The Money Unit was scrutinized by the writer, while it was being taught in two primary schools. This research had a number of objectives, some of which were relevant to the present investigation. Caution must be exercised in generalising from such a small sample, but, as will be seen from Chapter VIII, the sample was not small relative to the number of schools using the unit. It did seem that the unit failed to allow enough scope for development of teacher autonomy. Several examples were noted of lack of time even to complete the material, and to follow up suggestions made in the Teacher's Guide. Very little encouragement was given to deeper analysis of purpose, and where the unit contained suggestions for linking material with key concepts and objectives, it was easily by-passed.

The stated objectives for the unit do not match the Project Team's rationale for the use of objectives. In particular, stated unit objectives are overwhelmingly intellectual or cognitive in character, and almost completely restricted to achievement in the field of economics. Therefore there was little incentive to use to the full potentially rich material, which cut across several social science disciplines. As a result, some statements and conclusions, and the underlying attitudes which should have been questioned, were ignored.

Key concepts were intended to be used as a means of organising material to achieve objectives. But it was possible to ignore, almost totally, suggestions for relating lesson work to over-arching key concepts. Once immersion in the unit had been achieved, both over-arching concepts and objectives were lost in the minutiae of individual lessons.

It appears that the unit does not encapsulate project philosophy, but that on the contrary, it is possible for intelligent and experienced teachers to work through the unit without reference to the stated aims and concepts to be mastered. Moreover, the unit does not encourage or compel the teachers to think out their own objectives or what concepts they want their pupils to master. It cannot be assumed that such units will be used in any of the ways in which their originators intended or hoped.

2. Evaluation of the Content of the Unit in the Context of the primary school classroom

The inescapable conclusion of the investigation made by the present writer into the use of the Money Unit was that the kit contained too much information and required too much time. In order to complete the more routine parts of the unit, other parts of the work were sacrificed.

A claim made in Regan and Leithwood's book suggests that, in a typical primary school, teachers are not concerned with more than the 'design of interesting activities and some assessment of results'.[14] It was in fact possible to ignore almost completely the few suggestions made to utilize key concepts as tools to select content and to achieve objectives. No attempt was made to test against the objectives listed in the unit. Some continuous assessment of worksheet material and classroom activity occurred, but this was unstructured. If Regan and Leithwood's description given above is an accurate reflection of primary school activity, then the actual lessons using unit materials correspond closely with existing rationale. There was no conscious attempt in the unit to apply modern psychological theories of 'matching' or 'spiral development'. In fact, the transition to the stage where more variables were simultaneously manipulated was abrupt. The major factor inhibiting the use of materials as resources for individual use rather than in a prescriptive way was the actual quantity of work. Independent study, group learning, revision, remedial work and enrichment were eventually sacrificed in the cause of 'getting through the Unit'. In addition, even if time had allowed, there was still no means for matching pupils with appropriate materials.

However, these criticisms apply to this particular unit alone. Its deficiencies in reflecting project philosophy and in content presentation constitute constraints to its effectiveness, but they *may* be factors peculiar to this unit alone.

Conclusions

A. Some basic conditions must be met before a curriculum package may be expected to act as a means of diffusing project philosophy. First, the unit should adequately and correctly reflect project philosophy. Secondly, the study of the project pamphlets should be an integral part of the unit. This condition is particularly important if the first condition is inadequately satisfied. Thirdly, it should not be possible to ignore those sections of the unit which are particularly closely related to the project. On the contrary, these sections should be given greater weight.

B. Most curriculum development models have been means/ends ones. But teachers are not used to the idea of stating objectives, nor do they have appropriate training. Units which set limited objectives and which do not apply these rigorously merely reinforce existing practice.

C. Lack of observation and assessment techniques necessary before individual pupils can be 'matched' with material may be a general constraint impeding development, especially because of its inhibitory effect on teacher involvement in project philosophy.

Relevant in this context is the work of the *Progress in Learning Science* Project.[15] The purpose of this project is to help teachers gather information about their children's abilities, concepts and attitudes and make decisions about activities and approaches in the classroom based on this information. Since no two children will be alike in the various characteristics which are relevant to their learning, taking these characteristics into account means that children have to be thought of and catered for as individuals, not as groups or as a whole class.

In order to assist making decisions which

improve the matching of activities to children, the project produced two kinds of draft materials:

   (i) material to guide teachers in using their observations of children to pick up information which would help in matching;

  (ii) guides to choosing activities and to approaches which are likely to 'match' children at different points in their development of various characteristics (abilities, concepts and attitudes).

Each of the checklists consists of statements referring to the development of 25 or so characteristics relevant to 'science' activities. For each characteristic there are three statements describing children's activities or responses which are considered indicative of different levels of development.

The guides to diagnosis and development each relate to one of the characteristics on the checklists. These guides are intended to help in the *selection* of activities and not to describe activities in detail. Each one provides some description of how the particular concept or attitude develops, how development can be noticed in children's normal classroom activities, and suggests, often through examples provided by teachers, approaches and activities which promote progress in various points.

The author of this pamphlet[16] echoes the concern of the present writer: 'Preparation of materials is only part of the task of curriculum innovation, and preparation of teachers is required to complete the job'. It is clear that the project's products are not really effective unless teachers have a chance to discuss the ideas behind them, explore the implications for their own work and relate the ideas about matching and development to the children they know.

D. Trial stages inform teachers that they have to think differently. Kits do not; they may in fact mask this intended metamorphosis, unless constant critical evaluation is an integral part of the project.

References

1   Schools Council History, Geography and Social Science 8-13 Project: *Curriculum Planning in History, Geography and Social Science,* by the Research Team (Collins, 1976).

2   ibid., p.13.

3   ibid., p.35.

4   ibid., p.71.

5   ibid., p.88.

6   ibid., p.109.

7   Schools Council History, Geography and Social Science 8-13 Project: *An Interim Statement* (September, 1972), p.7.

8   Kingdom, E.F., *Key Concepts and Curriculum Content,* unpublished occasional paper for the History, Geography and Social Science 8-13 Project (1974), p.19.

9   ibid., p.20.

10 See note 7 above, p.15.

11 Kingdom, E.F., ibid., p.22.

12 ibid., p.25.

13 Blyth, W.A.L., Schools Council History, Geography and Social Science 8-13 Project: *Spotlights, a Summary of the Project's Approach* (unpublished Mimeo, 1973), p.26.

14 Regan, E.M. and Leithwood, K.A., *Effecting Curriculum Change – Experiences with the Conceptual Skills Project* (Ontario Institute for Studies in Education, 1974), p.1.

15 Schools Council Progress in Learning Science Project: *Information Paper No. 5* (September, 1975).

16 ibid., p.5.

CHAPTER VIII

SURVEY OF THE USE OF THE MONEY
UNIT

Introduction

A number of questions concerning the
dissemination and use of the Money Unit
have not yet been considered. For example,
to what extent did the project achieve its
goal of encouraging teachers to think
deeply, systematically and reflectively about
what they were doing? How many of the
project materials sold were actually used?
Of those used, how many were implemented
in the way in which the project intended?
Is it possible to distinguish varying degrees
in the application of the project's
philosophy? Is it realistic to expect teachers
to read or buy the project's background
and support publications, including
teachers' booklets? How were decisions to
adopt the project taken in different schools?
What constraints were there to the exercise
of 'informed choice'? What barriers to
implementation existed?

To ensure that over a period of time and
in the design of a sequence of units, no one
set of objectives was unduly neglected, the
Table of Objectives could be used. To what
extent *was* it used? Another problem was
whether the 'key concepts' enabled teachers
to see subject matter from a new and more
co-ordinated standpoint. Could the key
concepts be made operational in order to
act as a filter for curriculum content? Were
the objectives, concepts and materials kit
adapted by teachers to their unique
situation?

In order to make some attempt to answer
some of these questions, a small-scale survey
was designed and used. The publishers of
the Money Unit supplied a list of purchasers
of the Money Unit. Because of the small
numbers of schools that had bought the
unit (10 in the entire United Kingdom) a
questionnaire was used to canvass all of
them. In one case this was coupled with a
visit. The questionnaire was also sent to the
three teachers' centres and two other
organisations within the London area
which had bought the unit.

The questionnaire, devised by the writer,
is in some respects an adaptation of the
'End of Unit Report' used by the project
evaluator with trial schools and reported in
an Appendix to a Project paper.[1] The
questions asked were as follows:—

1. How did you find out about the
   Money Unit?
2. Have you used the unit with any
   class?
3. If so, please state size of class and
   average age of pupils.
4. Did you decide to use the unit mainly
   because it was interesting and
   stimulating material or because it
   presented the opportunity to use key
   concepts and objectives?
5. Did you use the entire unit?
6. If not, which parts did you omit and
   why?
7. Have you had any Economics
   training?

8. Did you specify any objectives before you started the unit? If so, what were they?

9. Which of the categories of objectives mentioned in the Teachers' Guide did you regard as most important?

10. Did you use any key concepts? If so, state which.

11. Did you find any parts of the unit useful in helping understanding of key concepts? If so, state which parts.

12. What did you expect the pupils to learn from the unit?

13. Did you find it easy to test whether they had done so?

14. If so, what procedures did you use? If so, please state reasons.

15. Have you read any of the project's publications other than those contained in the Money Unit?

16. Are you likely to use the Money Unit again?

Analysis of schools and other organisations surveyed

As stated above, all ten schools in the United Kingdom which had bought the Money Unit were surveyed. Of these, nine responded in some way to the request for information. In the case of the non-respondent, telephone calls and the sending of duplicate questionnaires failed to evoke any response.

Of the schools with which contact was made, five had used the unit in some way. One school replied that the unit had not in fact been purchased. In another, it was bought but not used. In two others, it was only the inspection copy material which had been ordered, and this had been returned.

School 1: Comprehensive School. For detailed analysis of interview with Head of Social Studies Department, see Appendix II.

School 2: Middle School. The teacher responding here felt that her answers were perhaps incoherent; she found the questions rather demanding. She said that she rarely rethought out her objectives and evaluated her work as thoroughly as she should. She had used some of the unit.

School 3: Junior School. The teacher responding stated that she had attempted to complete the questionnaire and had failed very badly. She was in sympathy with the aims and concepts of the project, but had to admit that her real reasons for trying to implement those objectives, using the material contained in the unit, were curiosity, and a feeling that such an expensive piece of equipment ought to be used by someone in the school. She wrote: 'Perhaps these reasons did not supply the necessary incentive to use properly the probably valuable suggestions contained in the unit. I must also state the particular format of the unit does not suit my general way of teaching, which is to work from the interests of the children, rather than impose interests on them.'

School 4: Comprehensive School. Did not purchase the Money Unit.

School 5: Junior Comprehensive School. The responding teacher bought the unit because it seemed to tie in with his theme on 'Shops and Shopping' which he was pursuing as part of an Environmental Studies course. He never intended to use the whole unit — merely to look for ideas which would fit in with his scheme. In the event he didn't teach on the course anyway, so he never used the unit.

School 6: Primary School. Ordered only the Inspection Copy material, and returned it unused. The school intended to bring History, Geography and Science together, not Economics. The school was involved in a Mathematics Project, and did not want to 'eat into' this time.

School 7: Primary School. No response.

School 8: Middle School. Returned the material because of staff changes and because other staff showed little enthusiasm.

School 9: Middle School. Was using the unit correctly.

School 10: Middle School. Had used the unit the previous year.

The other organisations surveyed were three teachers' centres, a University College, and a Polytechnic. One of the teachers' centres failed to respond. A second was a specialist maths teachers' centre. The unit had been bought for reference only; it could not be borrowed for use in a school. It was used by lecturers as an example of a multi-media pack, and it was frequently demonstrated on primary teachers' courses when the intention was to induce the teachers to construct their own multi-media packs. The centres had learnt about the unit through the publisher's catalogue. The other teachers' centre surveyed which had bought the unit reported that it had been borrowed by two student teachers who were developing a 2nd/3rd year programme for social studies. It was thought that they were preparing a syllabus, possibly using the materials. The unit had not yet been borrowed by any primary school teachers, or indeed anyone else. The Polytechnic did not respond. The University College had bought the unit for its History Department, where it remained unused.

Analysis of Questionnaire Responses

Although the number of schools surveyed was extremely small, it is possible to generalise about the responses since *all* schools who had bought the Money Unit were questioned. An attempt must be made to answer the queries raised in the introduction to this chapter. It is not possible to conclude from the responses to the questionnaire that the project achieved its goal of encouraging teachers to think deeply, systematically and reflectively about what they were doing. In the main the responses were superficial and there was a tendency, shown particularly by School 3, to evade the thought necessary to answer the more searching questions. It may be however that the questionnaire method encouraged superficial responses. Where it was administered by means of an interview, as in School 1, the response elicited was far more penetrating although this may, of course, just have been a personal difference. For detailed tabulation of the survey returns, see Appendix III.

The survey did help considerably to answer the question as to whether many of the materials sold had actually been used. Despite the fact that this was a national project, with considerable financial support, and despite all the efforts that the project team put into making the project more widely known, together with national advertising of the Money Unit, only *five* schools in the entire United Kingdom could be found where the unit had been or was being used. Moreover this result applies to one of the principal actual outputs of the project. If all the financial, physical and human resources involved only precipitate this outcome, surely the whole rationale of such curriculum development projects must be questioned. However, it could be argued that the evidence on the Money Unit may not be typical of the destiny of the other units produced by the project. This requires further investigation.

The next set of questions asked whether any of the materials that *were* being used were being implemented in the way the project intended, or whether it was possible to distinguish varying degrees in the application of project philosophy.

Similar questions asked whether the objectives were brought into play, and whether the key concepts were invoked at any stage, and whether the materials were adapted by teachers to their unique situation.

All those schools that responded to question 4 agreed that they decided to use the Money Unit because they thought it would be interesting and stimulating, and two of them said they used it also because it presented the opportunity to use key concepts and objectives. School 1 seemed to travel furthest in the direction of implementing project philosophy. It did select some key concepts as particularly relevant, and it did use the materials discriminatingly, just selecting what it anticipated would be interesting. School 2 omitted inappropriate material for the age-group being taught. School 3 thought one of the simulations too contrived, and School 9 cut out a lot of material because of the time constraint and because some of it seemed uninteresting or unnecessary. Only

two of the schools specified any objectives before starting the unit, and yet this is crucial in implementing project philosophy. One of these schools distinguished between cognitive and affective objectives. It stressed mainly intellectual skills, such as finding, interpreting and evaluating information, and then communicating results. But it wanted also to effect attitudes, by encouraging openness to differences in other peoples' way of life and values, and by developing empathy with them. This is probably the most explicit application of project ideas in the survey. The other school (9) that pre-specified objectives defined only economic concepts to be learnt.

The answers to question 9, about which categories of objectives mentioned in the Teachers' Guide the teacher found most important, illustrated that objectives were still very much regarded as incantatory rituals. All four schools responding emphasised cognitive objectives, but it appeared that none of them had been carefully considered in relation to the particular pupils being taught. Matching seems to have been wholly ignored.

The questions on key concepts (10 and 11) elicited the least helpful responses. One of the five schools did not even use any key concepts, whilst two others did not respond. Of those mentioning key concepts, one did not mention values, and neither listed power, despite the fact that these two substantive key concepts were stressed by the authors of the Money Unit as being particularly capable of being articulated through it. One school found most of the unit helpful in reinforcing the key concepts, whilst three did not respond.

From the project's point of view, perhaps the most disappointing answers were given to question 12. All teachers took learning to mean learning of *economic* concepts, and almost all the other possibilities as suggested in the Table of Objectives and key concepts were ignored. Only School 2 stressed wider understanding, such as 'insight into similarity/difference, with cross-cultural comparisons. Causes and consequences of some aspects of human behaviour etc.' Questions 13 and 14 asked about testing. Only School 1 raised the problem of individual assessment in mixed ability classes. It had had a teachers' meeting but this was more concerned with evaluating the material than with assessing the pupils. School 2 showed awareness that inadequate instruments were provided. The teacher could gain an intuitive awareness of how pupils' understanding was developing, but more rigorous procedures were needed. It was easier to test whether 'facts' had been assimilated than whether attitudes had been changed, for example. One school gave no response to either question on testing. The remaining two schools found testing easy, by means of class discussion, oral questioning and written work. It is not clear however whether the procedures they used were in fact effective.

Another question raised in the introduction to this chapter asked whether it was realistic to expect teachers to read or buy the project's background and support publications, including teachers' booklets. Although two teachers said that they *had* read other relevant publications, it is difficult to put too much weight on these responses, since they did not specify which publications they had read. Even in School 1, which had perhaps the keenest and most thoughtful user of project materials, the teacher was not prepared to buy the key book to help teachers gain some insight into project philosophy. Teachers had found out about the Money Unit in diverse ways. Two had read about it in advertisements or articles in the educational press,

and one of these had been introduced to it at a teachers' centre meeting. Two others had innocently come upon the unit in their school resources, and had decided to make use of it. The final school had been told about its existence by the project director.

Since schools which ordered inspection copies of the unit were not followed up, it was difficult to determine what constraints there were to the exercise of 'informed choice' and to ascertain what barriers to implementation existed. In conclusion to this treatment of the survey teams, it may be noted that only two of the five schools were very likely to use the materials in the Money Unit again.

Conclusions from the Survey

A. The Money Unit has had a negligible impact on United Kingdom schools. The return on the investment in developing a new awareness of social science for the 8-13 age group has been minimal.

B. Where the unit has been used, it has principally been regarded as a collection of possibly interesting material. Mostly the kit has not been regarded as an examplar of how to select materials using the objectives and key concepts as criteria and filters respectively.

C. The evidence obtained reinforces the conclusion in Chapter VII that far greater emphasis needs to be laid on dissemination, and on incorporating project philosophy into published materials.

References

1   Baranowski, M., *A Pilgrim's Progress through the Project*, occasional paper No.2, Schools Council History, Geography and Social Science 8-13 Project (1973), pp.39-40.

CHAPTER IX

OTHER EVIDENCE ON THE
DISSEMINATION OF INNOVATIONS

There have only been two recent general
studies of the extent to which teachers
know about and use curriculum
developments.

Do Headteachers know about Projects?

A research study by R.B. Nicodemus and
D. Marshall on the familiarity of headteachers with twenty-five new curriculum
projects was published in 1975.[1] The
investigation covered the period 1971-4,
and in the winter of 1972, they conducted
by means of a questionnaire a national
survey of headteachers (an 8% random
sample of headteachers in maintained
secondary schools excluding ILEA), and
made case studies of schools in four local
education authorities. The questionnaire
was designed to assess whether headteachers
knew about, or whether their schools used,
materials from twenty-five curriculum
projects funded by the Nuffield Foundation
and the Schools Council.

Of the 402 questionnaires distributed,
289 were returned. The answers revealed a
tremendous range both in knowledge and
use of projects' materials. For example,
whilst 82% of grammar school headteachers
had heard of Nuffield 'O' Level Chemistry,
only 11% of headteachers of secondary
modern schools were aware of the Schools
Council's Project Environment. Similarly,
the percentage of schools actually using
project materials (according to the head-

teachers) varied from 62% for Nuffield 'O'
Level Chemistry to 0% for the Schools
Council Integrated Science Project (in
grammar schools). Table 5 opposite provides
the complete picture on headteachers'
familiarity with and take-up of projects.
What stands out most clearly is the very
low average take-up of Schools Council
materials, compared with the Nuffield
Projects.

Nicodemus and Marshall also asked headteachers what they regarded as the most
useful sources of information about new
projects, and their responses are duplicated
in Table 6 on page 54. It transpired that the
most useful source was the individual Head
of Department in the school. In contrast,
impersonal or printed sources of information
were rated as very useful by less than half
the headteachers responding.

Other minor sources of information
included LEA circulars, other Schools
Council publications, and school governors.
Of the other 14 sources listed, nine were
still rated as useful, with about one-quarter
of responses in the category 'very useful'
and about one-half in the 'sometimes useful'
category. They were: headteachers, Times
Educational Supplement, Project Profiles
and Index, staff from schools participating
in the trials of a curriculum project,
specialist subject journals, teachers from
other schools, BBC TV educational
programmes, HMI, information from
publishers.

Only five sources could be considered

Table 5

	Percentage of Headteachers aware of New Projects' Existence			Percentage of Headteachers reporting adoption of project materials			
	GM	SM	CO	GM	SM	CO	Ave. Total %
N =	61	123	96	61	123	96	289
Projects Supported by the Schools Council							
Environmental Studies	66	54	64	5	11	10	10
General Studies Project	64	34	59	21	4	12	11
Humanities Curriculum Project	57	67	82	8	33	35	29
Integrated Science	49	32	57	0	1	2	1
Keele Integrated Studies	30	27	38	2	2	2	2
Loughborough Engineering Science	24	13	26	2	1	1	1
Mathematics for the Majority	36	50	56	0	7	11	7
" " " Continuation Project	15	21	27	2	6	3	4
Midlands Mathematics Experiment	43	32	40	5	2	5	4
Moral Education 13-16	46	36	50	5	3	7	5
N-W Regional Curriculum Development Project	18	28	31	5	7	8	7
Project Environment	13	11	18	0	0	0	0
Project Technology	51	43	56	15	6	18	12
Science 5-13	18	20	28	0	0	0	0
Nuffield Projects							
O-Level Biology	79	51	80	61	18	40	34
O-Level Chemistry	82	48	79	62	8	38	30
O-Level Physics	80	50	79	59	12	42	32
A-Level Biological Science	67	19	47	25	1	6	8
A-Level Chemistry	77	20	54	31	1	9	10
A-Level Physics	72	20	57	23	1	7	8
A-Level Physical Science	54	19	47	2	0	0	0
Combined Science	57	58	62	10	33	30	27
Secondary Science	43	53	61	2	27	21	19
Nuffield Mathematics	59	37	55	3	10	9	8
Other							
Scottish Integrated Science	5	11	17	0	2	5	2

GM = Grammar Schools;   SM = Secondary Modern Schools;   CO = Comprehensive Schools.

Source: Nicodemus, R.B. and Marshall, D. *op. cit.*

useless, in so far as more than 50% of the responses were in categories '2' and '1'. They were: information from supply catalogues, Schools Council Field Officers, college of education lecturers, parents, university lecturers.

Finally, the responses to the questionnaire indicated what factors helped or hindered the adoption of a project's materials. More than half of the headteachers thought that the following facilitators were important: LEA initiative in innovation; LEA advisory service; active teachers' centre in the area; contact between schools in the area; qualifications of teaching staff.[2] However, the majority of headteachers thought that reasons why materials were frequently not adopted included: overworked staff; lack of money to launch or maintain projects, and inadequate accommodation in the school.

The Schools Council – A Self-Assessment

The Impact and Take-up Project published an Interim Report in 1978.[3] This provides analyses of responses to a questionnaire posted to 479 primary schools in 1977. Both these surveys were conducted across England and Wales.

Essentially the aim of the investigation was to find out how familiar teachers were with the ideas and materials of 44 projects aimed at primary and middle schools, and to what extent they used them.

The report is justifiably cautious in interpreting the survey findings. It might be that teachers were using project materials for ideas, without realising their origin. Some projects had finished their work some time ago, and teachers might find it difficult to remember exactly what factors influenced their decision whether to use them or not. Some might not be aware that

Table 6

Usefulness of Sources for Information about curriculum development projects

% of Headteachers responding to code categories (N = 289)

Rank	Code:	4	3	2	1
1. Head of Department in your School		66	32	2	0
2. Information direct from curriculum development projects		45	47	8	0
3. Schools Council: 'Dialogue'		40	50	8	1
4. Assistant teachers in your School		34	54	10	2
5. LEA Advisers/Inspectors		33	44	19	4
6. DES memoranda and circulars		26	60	12	2

Code: 4 – very useful; 3 – sometimes useful; 2 – rarely useful; 1 – never useful.
Source: ibid.

the curriculum they are teaching in fact evolved as a result of the influence of a project on a member of staff whom they have now replaced. Of the approach sample of 479 schools (random sample, stratified by school size and type, and supplied by DES), 308 returned at least one questionnaire (64 per cent return rate). The estimated return rate within schools was 60 per cent.

Headteachers were asked to say how many of 16 Schools Council and Nuffield Projects which had published materials for primary schools by the end of December 1976 were in use in the school at the time of the survey. According to them, between

81 and 85 per cent of primary schools were using at least one of the 16 listed projects. Around 43 to 47 per cent of primary schools were using one or two projects and about 37 per cent were using three or more.

Observers saw project teaching materials in about four-fifths of the 107 schools visited, though little weight should be placed on this statistic. Materials on the History, Geography and Social Science 8-13 Project were seen in three schools. Altogether materials from 19 projects were observed. These fall into two groups. The first group, of nine projects, is known by 42 to 80 per cent of headteachers (i.e. they have read part of the materials or are well acquainted with the project) and these projects are (except ita) reported to be used in 15 to 50 per cent of schools. These projects are: Breakthrough, SRA,* Nuffield Maths, Science 5-13, Mathematics in Primary Schools, Communication Skills (3-7), En Avant, Nuffield Junior Science, ita.

The second group of projects is known by only 7 to 20 per cent of heads, and they are used in less than 10 per cent of the schools. The projects in this group are: Art and Craft, 'Check-Ups', Environmental Studies, Music Education (3-11), History, Geography and Social Science 8-13, Project Environment, Science and Mathematical Concepts, Man: A Course of Study, (Scope), (Concept 7-9).

The survey of teachers showed similar results. Less than nine per cent had heard of any projects in the second group and less than six per cent had used any of them.

The Interim Report proceeds to

*SRA stands for Science Research Associates Ltd, a publisher of a laboratory approach to reading and other skills which originated in North America. It is not connected with Schools Council or Nuffield projects.

summarise results for each project. Some of these findings are worth highlighting. A number of instances are given where a project had no time specifically allocated for dissemination *after* published materials were available. For example, the dissemination activities of the Environmental Studies Project *accompanied* the production of materials and it is perhaps not surprising that the survey revealed that the project had only influenced three per cent of primary teachers, and only three per cent were using its materials or ideas with one per cent having used them in the past.

One project which is shown to have benefited from the increased emphasis that the Schools Council has placed on dissemination since 1972-3 is the Music Education of Young Children Project. A Centre for Continued Dissemination has been set up at Reading University. Although at the time of the survey, the first wave of this project's materials had only just come on the market, 37 per cent of headteachers had heard of it.

Another project with a systematic dissemination phase was Science 5-13, which attempted to set up a network of schools which would provide the nucleus for dissemination at the end of the project. Since 1975 (the end of the project) nine Area Liaison Officers have helped this process in England and Wales. Furthermore, materials were published well before the end of the project's life and a survey shows that almost half of all primary teachers were familiar with the project, and almost a quarter were using it.

The questionnaire also asked teachers how familiar they were with other Schools Council publications. Even the best known — 'The Language of Primary School Children' and 'Gifted Children in Primary Schools' — were known by less than 40 per cent of teachers. The Report comments delicately that 'Primary school teachers are largely unaware of the existence of the reports, working papers, research studies etc published by the Schools Council, and the majority of headteachers are unaware of all but three of the twenty-five publications listed. If these headteachers and teachers are the intended audience for these publications, and judging by statements upon the publications themselves this is certainly the case, then this is a less than satisfactory state of affairs.' (Page 75.) The Interim Report concludes with a summary of five points for discussion. The first is that it is not possible for teachers to make effective choices unless they know what is on offer. Eighty per cent of heads and more than ninety per cent of teachers have not had any contact with half the listed projects or their materials. So it appears that many projects are not communicating their information to heads or teachers sufficiently adequately for them even to consider whether or not to adopt them.

Secondly, it may be that headteachers and teachers do not consider that Schools Council publications (other than project materials and ideas) are written for them. If this is the case, writers will need to consider their target audience more carefully.

Thirdly, projects tend to be given up mainly when teachers move or are promoted, though incoming teachers are often asked by heads to continue with them. Thought needs to be given on how to keep projects going despite teacher mobility.

With regard to the sources of information about projects, it is significant that for both headteachers and teachers, short courses/conferences and teachers' centres appear most important and useful. But given that information about Schools

Council projects is not percolating through to the schools via these well used channels, is it not time for the Schools Council to consider whether perhaps some other channel should be developed? The Report stresses that the Schools Council may be able to explore the use of television and radio to tell teachers about projects. Another suggestion is that the educational press might be used more purposefully. The Schools Council could regularly take advertising space in, for example, the Times Educational Supplement to advertise projects aimed at a specific age range or curriculum area.

Lastly, although the initial contact with projects comes when teachers are in training, it is important for LEAs to make a serious commitment to in-service training, so that a continuous opportunity for disseminating information about Schools Council projects is provided.

The implication behind much of the Interim Report is that it is regrettable, to say the least, that more teachers have not availed themselves of Schools Council project materials and ideas. However, might it not be that, through informal contacts, teachers gain a fairly good idea of the likely relevance (or lack of it) of certain projects to their own needs? If some projects are thought not to be worth taking seriously, this would account for the lack of take-up. But this consideration would not meet the point that teachers are on the whole ignorant of the existence of projects, and so not in a very strong position to pronounce on the usefulness or relevance of any particular project to their needs.

In conclusion, it is ironic to note how persons connected with the Schools Council, leading union representatives and similar 'functionaries' reacted to the Interim Report. Mostly they were pleased and encouraged by the findings, and stress that they had no desire to impose projects on teachers, who had every right to decide for themselves. But it is difficult for an impartial observer to share their optimism, unless steps are taken to implement some of the sensible suggestions for improving dissemination strategy outlined in the report.

References

1   Nicodemus, R.B. and Marshall, D., 'Familiarity of Headteachers with Twenty-five New Curriculum Projects' in *Educational Studies*, Vol.1 No.3, October 1975, pp.191-200.
2.   ibid., p.197.
3   Steadman, S.D. *et al.*, Impact and Take-up Project: *A First Interim Report to the Programme Committee of the Schools Council* (Schools Council, May 1978).

CHAPTER X

CONCLUSIONS

1. General Problems of Dissemination

If the dissemination phase of a curriculum development project is to be successful, it needs to be organised methodically on a large scale. It cannot be left to chance, *laissez faire* or an expectation that teachers will eagerly research all new materials. Without such a pattern of dissemination, it is unlikely that schools will voluntarily take up innovations and use them in the way in which the originators intended. Probably, at least as many resources need to be devoted to this phase as to the development of resources phase, in terms of time, money and personnel. A major purpose of the dissemination phase should be to bring about desired changes in teachers' approaches by means of induction courses and training programmes, not only where new curriculum content is involved, but also where there are radical changes in teaching style expected. It is unlikely that curriculum developers' hortatory remarks will change teaching practices.

The end-product of most projects is kits of materials. These are often just intended to serve as examplars, but they will be treated as definitive and prescriptive unless they are so structured that the teacher is compelled to re-assess his teaching strategies. One way of doing this would be to incorporate documents outlining project philosophy into the materials, rather than providing them as expensive optional extras.

No project is likely to succeed unless it takes into account possible motives on the part of the teacher in adopting it. Such developments are more likely to take place if they have a beneficial effect on the teacher's status, promotion prospects or earnings. Additionally, although local teacher meetings would be very helpful in encouraging the cross-fertilization of ideas, and in dissemination, they are unlikely to be very successful unless they are held within school time and teachers perceive them to be of practical utility. This necessitates commitment of the local authority to the innovation, and provision of facilities for the release of teachers for in-service (re-)training.

In order that teachers may inspect the full range of projects available, regional information centres and curriculum development centres should be set up. These would also act as foci for teachers taking part in development groups for local projects. Finally, judgements about dissemination practices would be more substantial if criteria were developed for evaluating their effectiveness.

2. Conclusions on the Money Unit

A project is unlikely to succeed if teachers anticipate that they will be out of their depth in using it. It is much more likely to be taken up if it appears to fit in easily with existing subjects, practices and teachers' requirements. The time constraint will often inhibit the development of links between a new unit and other school subjects. There is a tendency for an over-abundance of material to constrain rather than liberate the teacher.

Any innovation whose use implies a revolution in teachers' practices is unlikely to succeed, whether or not it conceals from teachers initially that it has this implication. The Money Unit of the HGSS 8-13 Project did not encapsulate project philosophy, and experienced teachers could work through the unit without reference to the stated aims and concepts to be mastered. It seems that teachers at large cannot be expected to use the materials in the same way as teachers in the 'trial' stages of a project's life, who have access to project personnel and have been exposed fairly deeply to project philosophy. This conclusion is lent weight by the finding that only five schools in the entire United Kingdom had been using the Money Unit, most of which were not using it in the way in which the project team had hoped.

If teachers are intended to tailor curriculum materials to individual pupils' needs, they need to be provided with observation and assessment techniques capable of 'matching' materials and methods to pupils. But such techniques cannot simply be added to project material in the hope that they will be used. Some familiarisation programme, such as that used by the *Progress in Learning Science* Project, seems essential. Finally, some projects may be counter-productive. If a project is taken on by a teacher, who then begins to find it increasingly difficult to operate, or who gradually loses faith in it, this may cause him gradually to become disenchanted with curriculum development projects in general, and encourage him to feel justified in reverting to his former practices.

3. Possible Lines of Future Research

There are a number of ways in which the effectiveness of dissemination strategies might be evaluated. One method would be concurrent evaluation, similar to the formative evaluation of the curriculum development itself. Another possibility would be to group together projects with common elements, and appoint evaluators to work simultaneously with them. It would be helpful to have intensive studies of particular dissemination techniques, so that they could be assessed for the benefit of future projects. Further analytical studies and case histories could be based on the ideas of summative evaluation. More needs to be known about how decisions to adopt projects are taken, how the exercise of 'informed choice' is constrained, and what prevents positive decisions from being implemented.

Finally with respect to the HGSS 8-13 Project, it would be valuable to establish how closely the implementation pattern conformed to that predicted by the project team, and it would be interesting to know whether the other units were more successful.

APPENDIX I

Findings of the Impact and Take-up Project with respect to the HGSS 8-13 Project

| | *Familiarity* | | | |
	Don't know of	Read of or Heard of	Read Parts	Know well
	%	%	%	%
Headteachers*	68	20	7	4
Teachers of 8-13 year olds	86	9	3	1
All primary teachers	91	5	2	1

| | *Teacher Use* | | |
	Influenced	Using	Have Used
	%	%	%
Teachers of 8-13 year olds	3	2	1

| | *School Use* (according to Heads) | | |
	Considered	Using	Have Used
	%	%	%
Schools with junior age pupils	12	3	0

n = 191

* In schools with pupils aged 8-13.

Roughly a third (31%) of headteachers in schools with 8-13 year old pupils know of the project. Eleven per cent have read part of the materials, and the headteachers report that 3% of schools use the project. The materials were seen in about 3% of the visited schools. 3% of teachers of 8-13 year olds have been influenced by the project and 2% say they use it.

APPENDIX II

Interview with Head of Social Science Department at a Comprehensive School – 24.2.77

Q. How did you find out about the Money Unit?

A. Possibly through publicity – materials coming to the school, but at the same time they ran a course at the teachers' centre at Clapham, so I went along to that as well. But I was briefed beforehand. I'd also been to a Stoke d'Abernon course two years ago and I'd had a conversation with a Senior Research Officer of the Project. At the Clapham meeting, the advisory teacher showed the materials – what the pack contained, and we saw the filmstrips etc.

I initially saw the Inspection Copy materials – which the publishers are not particularly keen on giving you – I don't know why. I sent off for some inspection copy material on the Curriculum Planning book and they said no, it was on a cash or return basis.

Q. Have you run the Money Unit at all?

A. Yes, we're running it now, with second years, since last September. We're teaching it to every girl in the second year (390 girls) – rather we're using the materials rather than teaching it as a pack, you know, in the way in which they want it to be used, as stimulus material for teachers. We've fitted it into our framework. We've developed a second and third year course – two periods per week in the second year and three periods in the third year, and we're trying

to get lots of things together, and at the moment it's taking units and extracting what we want from them. But with the Money Unit, we've run it right through. I think we would alter it next year, especially the Tikopea bit. I felt the booklet was designed for a primary school; we needed very much more back-up material. We have got the Firth books and are making our own material from them, using the Tikopea booklet as a reader. I think you have to teach something first and you have to play it by ear.

Q. How many teachers are involved?

A. Five. We have one set of materials and a very good photo-copying machine. We've bought 100 Tikopea books. All the teachers get the Introduction to Place, Time and Society, and the Money Unit Teachers' Guide. We have two sets of the tape and filmstrip.

Q. Why did you decide to use the Money Unit?

A. We wanted to establish some ideas lower down the school, so that we could develop them in the fourth and fifth years.

Q. Did you want to use it because the material was interesting and stimulating, or because it gave you an opportunity to develop key concepts and objectives?

A. Well, I think it was both really. We picked out some key concepts – exchange, division of labour. *I* had to do this really, because we've had so many changes of staff. I like the way it says that these are here for you to use in the way you want, and you can therefore develop parallel information to go with it.

Q. Is it taking the right amount of time, roughly?

A. We've been doing it since September (one and a half terms). We spent quite a time on 'Survival'. It was the first time we'd taught mixed ability, so we wanted class-based lessons for a while. We developed 'Survival' for about six weeks and we had a lot of back-up stuff – the book 'Walkabout' and 'Lord of the Flies' – how people in groups survive – so we extended that section of it – and we only went on to the Tikopea section after half term. I anticipate that it will take two terms in all. This half term we're getting on to the Measure of Value section and we're using the TV programme put out by ITV as well – Meeting Our Needs.

Q. Did you use the Table of Objectives at all?

A. I think that everyone reading it through would say 'yes, I feel like this, but now I want to get on and teach it'. We didn't sit down in advance and specify objectives. I like the project's attitude from reading the introduction, but I then just wanted to get on and develop the course.

Q. Does anyone in your department have an Economics background?

A. We've all got Economics in our degrees – at least three of us.

Q. Which of the categories of objectives did you find most important?

A. I think these are all things which we haven't necessarily viewed in exactly the same way, but have said in department meetings. It's the way we teach social science in this school. We always are coming up against the question of kids finding and using information and then being able to interpret and evaluate it.

Q. Which key concepts did you want to stress?

A. Values and beliefs, communication, similarity and difference. The study sheet of definitions of money – where the notes fell off the back of a lorry – they found much too abstract to cope with. It helped to use a photo from Firth's book, 'We, the Tikopea', of one of the characters who is being quoted. I don't think the Tikopea booklet directs you to money in any particular way.

Q. Do you go through the unit religiously?

A. Absolutely no. We're really using the interesting material the way I want to – sometimes as back-up. I might use some of the ideas then and make my own worksheets. I suppose people can fall back on teaching it in the traditional way if they want to – this is useful to new teachers – who go very religiously through it. What I've done is to go through it, and then produce my own 'teachers' worksheet' for everyone in my department from it, saying how I would use various things – saying you've got the book and my worksheet – now use it how you want it. I had so many new teachers; in a couple of years it will probably be much more of a group effort. At first you have to guide them, make them feel secure and they can then go on. One of the new teachers began producing her own materials.

Q. What do you expect pupils to learn from this unit?

A. Needs, resources, division of labour – starting to look at the jobs people do – wages and salaries – the introduction to various words.

Q. Have you found it easy to test whether they have learnt what you want them to learn?

A. It's all tied up at the moment with assessing mixed ability. I don't say we're doing it yet, but everybody's talking about it. We did have a test at the end of last term – for straightforward learning things obviously. They got a bit confused about how the Tikopeans used money. When we talked about the Tikopeans going abroad, they tended to think it meant going on holiday, rather than going off to work in another country, and needing that money to support them. I'm also unhappy about the David White extract — where to use it. It's a very good idea and the kids responded to it quite well but I think I would put it later on. But they all grasped the basic point about trust. The other thing which I did with them (no one else in my department did) was the games. The 'Let's Swap' was difficult — they all wanted impossible things. The colditz game went down well. They were very, very good at bargaining! The less experienced teachers were rather hesitant to use them!

The only other kind of evaluation is that we've had teachers' meetings, where we have looked at books and considered what kids have said.

Q. Have you got any other Project publications?
A. We've got 'Life in the 30's'. They've sent me the inspection copy material on 'People on the Move'. I wanted to get hold of Curriculum Planning and other teachers' books — I tried to get hold of them by asking for inspection copies from the publishers and I got a letter saying no. This made me feel narky; I've got the pack etc. and I thought they could at least send me the inspection copy material first. I'm not going to pay £3.50 till I've seen it. I'd probably send off for the others. I wish they'd get a move on with doing some of the other things — Ceremonies, Family Choice.
Q. Will you use it again?
A. Definitely yes. It will become part of our second year course; our teachers like using it. We'll alter it each year — but they like the approach and the chance it has given to go through some of the ideas.

APPENDIX III:

Table of Survey Returns on Use of Money Unit

	School 1	School 2	School 3	School 9	School 10
Q. 1:	Publicity & teachers' centre course	Times Educational Supplement and Dialogue	Discovered in the school resources	In the school	From the Project Director at Liverpool University
2:	Yes	Yes	Yes	Yes	Yes
3:	Not known. 13/14	Five classes of 30. 11.	33. 10/11	27. 10/11	30. 12/13
4:	Both really. We picked out some key concepts	Both. I was looking for material to help organise a topic to best advantage. 'Money' I felt was an interesting subject.	NR	Interest and stimulation	Interesting and stimulating
5:	No. Just the interesting materials — the worksheets	No	No	No	Yes
6:	Not specified	The more juvenile worksheets	Shipwreck simulation as it is alien to my views on drama and thus alien to the children's previous experience	Phase 2 and barter game. Latter did not seem very interesting or necessary. Former was too detailed given that money was only a sub-section of a Humanities course on trade.	NR
7:	Yes. At least 3 ex 5 teachers have economics in their degrees	Yes	No	A little	'A' Level economics
8:	No	Yes, mainly intellectual skills. Finding, interpreting, evaluating information; the ability to communicate findings. Also I wanted to encourage an openness to differences in other people's way of life and values to exercise empathy	NR	Knowledge of self sufficiency & specialisation. Need for money as a medium of exchange as people become increasingly specialised.	No

	School 1	School 2	School 3	School 9	School 10
Q. 9:	We had differing views. Kids need to find information and use it, then interpret and evaluate it	Intellectual	NR	Ability to organise information through the use of concepts and generalisations	To try and inform the children that money was not the only form of currency
10:	Value and beliefs, communication, similarity and difference	Interdependence. Similarity/ difference and consequences	NR	No	NR
11:	NR	Most	NR	NR	Yes, the tape and films were useful
12:	Needs, resources, division of labour. Starting to look at the jobs people do. Wages and salaries — introduction to various words	Greater understanding of need for a 'money system'. Insight into similarity/differences — cross cultural comparisons. Causes and consequences of aspects of human behaviour etc.	NR	See Q.8	That money in our society was important, but that it was not for other societies in other parts of the world
13:	Problem of assessing mixed ability. One test	No	NR	Yes	Yes
14:	Teachers' meeting, where we looked at books and considered what kids had said	Find 'testing' difficult. Aware of 'flashes of insight' particularly in simulation/games. Can test 'facts assimilated' but not attitude change etc.	NR	Class discussion & written work	Questions — oral & written, at the end of the series of lessons
15:	No. Publishers would not send inspection copies.	Yes	NR	No	Yes
16:	Definitely yes	Yes	No	No	Possibly